# Teaching Study Skills and Strategies in High School

# Related Titles of Interest

**Teaching Study Skills and Strategies in College**
Patricia Iannuzzi, Stephen S. Strichart, and Charles T. Mangrum II
ISBN: 0-205-26817-X

**Active Learning: 101 Strategies to Teach Any Subject**
Mel Silberman
ISBN: 0-205-17866-9

**Teaching Study Skills and Strategies in Grades 4–8**
Charles T. Mangrum II, Patricia Iannuzzi, and Stephen S. Strichart
ISBN: 0-205-19879-1

**Teaching Study Strategies to Students with Learning Disabilities**
Stephen S. Strichart and Charles T. Mangrum II
ISBN: 0-205-13992-2

For more information or to purchase a book, please call 1-800-278-3525.

# Teaching Study Skills and Strategies in High School

**STEPHEN S. STRICHART**
*Florida International University*

**CHARLES T. MANGRUM II**
*University of Miami*

**PATRICIA IANNUZZI**
*Florida International University*

**Allyn and Bacon**
Boston   London   Toronto   Sydney   Tokyo   Singapore

**Library of Congress Cataloging-in-Publication Data**

Strichart, Stephen S.
    Teaching study skills and strategies in high school / Stephen S.
Strichart, Charles T. Mangrum II, Patricia Iannuzzi.
        p.    cm.
    ISBN 0-205-19881-3
    1. Study skills—Handbooks, manuals, etc.   2. Note-taking—
Handbooks, manuals, etc.   3. Library orientation—Handbooks,
manuals, etc.   4. High school students—Handbooks, manuals, etc.
I. Mangrum, Charles T.   II. Iannuzzi, Patricia.   III. Title.
LB1601.S77   1997
373.13'028'1—dc21                                    96-54830
                                                      CIP

Printed in the United States of America

10 9 8 7 6 5 4 3 2 1      01 00 99 98 97

# Contents

**CHAPTER TWO**

**Reading and Taking Notes from Textbooks        22**

**CHAPTER THREE**

**Taking Notes in Class        45**

**CHAPTER FOUR**

**Using the Library and the Internet to Locate Information  72**

**CHAPTER SEVEN**
## Writing a Research Paper        **154**

# Introduction

## HOW THIS BOOK WILL HELP

This book provides opportunities for active learning in the classroom. The reproducible activities will help students master study skills and strategies important for success in many subject areas. Teaching students to use study skills and strategies effectively is an important step in transforming dependent learners into independent learners. The activities are designed to help high school students become independent learners in an increasingly technology-based learning environment.

Accompanying this book is a trial version of a computer assessment titled *Study Skills and Strategies Assessment-High School Level* (3S-HS). 3S-HS assesses students' use of the study skills and strategies taught in this book. The free trial disk, available in Windows only, allows you to administer 3S-HS to five students. After five administrations, the trial disk is no longer usable. You may then purchase a disk with either 50 or an unlimited number of administrations in either Windows or Macintosh versions. The order form is found at the end of this book.

## THE STUDY SKILLS AND STRATEGIES OF HIGH SCHOOL STUDENTS

Many authors have described the study skills and strategies of high school students. When summarized, their conclusions are that many high school students:

1. Have little knowledge of effective techniques useful for remembering information learned from teachers and textual materials
2. Have underdeveloped study strategies for obtaining, organizing, and recording important information from textbooks
3. Do not have a system for taking notes from class presentations
4. Are not sufficiently familiar with print, electronic, and other sources of information found in today's libraries
5. Do not make adequate use of reference books and other sources of information which can further enhance their learning

6. Do not make use of the visual aids found in textual materials
7. Have incomplete knowledge on how to conduct library research and write a research paper
8. Do not know how to prepare for and take the common forms of tests administered in high school
9. Do not know how to organize their study time and their study place to maximize the opportunity for learning

## STUDY SKILLS AND STRATEGIES TAUGHT IN THIS BOOK

The study skills and strategies taught in this book are those most important for success in high school. The bibliography at the end of this book lists the sources we used along with our knowledge and experience to create the reproducible activities. The skills and strategies are presented in nine chapters, as follows:

**Chapter One. Remembering Information.** Learning something is of little value if what is learned cannot be recalled whenever necessary. In this chapter we present strategies high school students can use to retain the important information and ideas they learn from their teachers and textual materials.

**Chapter Two. Reading and Taking Notes from Textbooks.** Much of the information students must learn in high school is contained in their subject area textbooks. Students must be taught how to obtain information from their subject area textbooks effectively and efficiently. To do so, students must have a textbook reading and notetaking strategy. In this chapter students are taught to use a textbook reading and notetaking strategy called SQ3R.

**Chapter Three. Taking Notes in Class.** High school students must be taught effective ways to write down the important information presented by their teachers. In this chapter students are taught a strategy for taking class notes.

**Chapter Four. Using the Library and the Internet.** High school students must be taught to make appropriate use of the many print and electronic resources found in libraries. In this chapter we present strategies students can use to search for information using these resources.

**Chapter Five. Using Reference Sources.** High school students must be made aware of the many reference sources they can use to achieve success in school. In this chapter students are taught strategies for using both print and electronic forms of the following reference sources: dictionary, encyclopedia, thesaurus, almanac, and atlas.

**Chapter Six. Interpreting Visual Aids.** High school students must be taught how to interpret maps, graphs, diagrams, tables, and charts to increase their understanding of information found in textual materials. In this chapter we present strategies for interpreting these visual aids.

**Chapter Seven. Writing a Research Paper.** High school students must be able to do library research and write a research paper. They must be taught to obtain, document, and organize print and electronic information and present it in a clear written form. In this chapter students are taught a series of strategic steps to follow when writing a research paper.

**Chapter Eight. Preparing for and Taking Tests.** High school students must demonstrate mastery of information by successfully taking tests given in different formats. Many times students have learned information but lack the test preparation and test taking skills needed to demonstrate their knowledge. In this chapter students are taught a five-day strategy for preparing for tests. They are also taught how to do well on the following types of tests: multiple choice, true/false, matching, completion, and essay.

**Chapter Nine. Using Time and Space.** High school students have many demands on their time. They must make effective use of their time to complete school assignments and prepare adequately for tests. They must also have a good place to study. In this chapter students are taught strategies for scheduling their time and organizing their study space.

## HOW THIS BOOK IS ORGANIZED

Each chapter is organized as follows:

1. Objectives
2. Titles of Reproducible Activities
3. Using the Reproducible Activities
4. Reproducible Activities
5. Mastery Assessment
6. Answers for Reproducible Activities

## HOW TO USE THIS BOOK

1. Use the results from 3S-HS to select the chapters most appropriate for your students.
2. Duplicate the reproducible activities you wish to use.
3. Use the suggestions found in Using the Reproducible Activities and your own ideas to provide instruction.
4. Have students complete the Mastery Assessment at any point you feel they have learned the study skills and strategies presented in a chapter.

## TEACHING NOTES

Here are some things to do when using this book:

1. Go beyond the reproducibles to provide your students with additional practice in the use of the strategies. It is additional practice with materials that are directly related to classroom objectives that will enable students to achieve greater success in school.

2. Have the students use a study strategy under your supervision until they have mastered it. Mastery of a strategy means that students are able to recall it as rapidly as they can recall their own names or phone numbers. Mastery also means the ability to apply the strategy automatically to school tasks. Students have achieved mastery when they can automatically recall and apply a strategy. Until they have achieved this automaticity, there is no mastery.

3. Share the strategies with colleagues who also teach your students, and encourage your colleagues to have the students use the strategies in their classes as well. This will help to ensure that students generalize and maintain their use of the strategies.

4. Although the various study strategies are presented individually in this book, in reality students will need to use a combination of strategies to complete most assignments. For example, students studying for a test should use strategies for remembering information, reading textbooks, and managing time, in addition to test taking strategies. Use every opportunity to demonstrate or explain to your students how to combine the use of the various strategies presented in this book.

5. Motivate your students to want to use the study strategies taught in this book. We recommend you use the PARS motivation strategy developed by Forgan and Mangrum (1980). This strategy has four components: Purpose, Attitude, Results, Success.

   *Purpose.* Students are more likely to want to learn a study strategy when they understand how the strategy can help them succeed in school. Be sure to explain how its use can help them acquire more information and get better grades in your class and in their other classes.

   *Attitude.* Your attitude is infectious. If you are enthusiastic about a study strategy, your enthusiasm will transfer to your students, who are then likely to model your positive attitude toward the use of the strategy.

   *Results.* It is important to give students feedback on how well they are applying a strategy. The feedback needs to be very specific so that students understand what they did correctly and what they did wrong. Students need specific feedback in order to know what to do to improve their use of each strategy.

   *Success.* It is important that students experience success in the application of a strategy. Nothing elicits recurrent behavior as well as success.

6. Have students work cooperatively in pairs or small groups to practice applying the strategies to class assignments. Students can take turns demonstrating how a strategy is used or providing feedback on the effectiveness of its use.

# Acknowledgments

We express our appreciation to our colleagues at the University of Miami and Florida International University who graciously gave their time to review the activities in this book. Their reactions and recommendations were of great assistance to us. We also wish to acknowledge our university students, most of whom are classroom teachers. Feedback from their trial use of the activities in their classrooms allowed us to make important improvements.

# About the Authors

**Stephen S. Strichart** is professor of special education and learning disabilities at Florida International University, Miami, Florida. He graduated from the City College of New York and taught children with various types of disabilities before entering graduate school. Dr. Strichart earned a Ph.D. from Yeshiva University in 1972. Since 1975 he has been on the faculty at Florida International University, where he trains teachers and psychologists to work with exceptional students. Dr. Strichart is the author of many books and articles on topics related to special education and study skills.

**Charles T. Mangrum II** is professor of special education and reading at the University of Miami, Coral Gables, Florida. He graduated from Northern Michigan University and taught elementary and secondary school before entering graduate school. He earned a Ed.D. from Indiana University in 1968. Since 1968 he has been on the faculty at the University of Miami, where he trains teachers who teach students with reading and learning disabilities. Dr. Mangrum is the author of many books, instructional programs, and articles on topics related to reading and study skills.

**Patricia Iannuzzi** is University Librarian and Head of the Reference Department at Florida International University Libraries. She graduated from Yale University and earned an M.S. in Library and Information Science at Simmons College in 1980. Ms. Iannuzzi has worked in libraries at Tufts University, Yale University, and the University of California at Berkeley. Since 1991 she has been on the library faculty at Florida International University, where she manages reference services, develops information literacy curricula, and teaches information literacy skills in subjects across the curriculum.

Teaching Study Skills
and Strategies
in High School

## CHAPTER ONE

# Remembering Information

## CHAPTER OBJECTIVES

1. Teach students a strategy for remembering information.
2. Teach students to use a variety of techniques to remember information.

## TITLES OF REPRODUCIBLE ACTIVITIES

## USING THE REPRODUCIBLE ACTIVITIES

After you have distributed a reproducible activity, here are suggestions for its use. Feel free to add further information, illustrations, or examples. Wherever possible, relate the activity to actual subject area assignments.

## 1-1   Selecting What You Need to Remember

Discuss the importance of remembering information. Tell students they will learn how to use a remembering strategy: (1) selecting information to be remembered and (2) using techniques to remember information. Discuss the guidelines for selecting information to be remembered. Then have students complete the activity.

## 1-2   Using Visualization to Remember Information

Visualization involves creating one or more mental images or pictures, which are later used to recall information. The mental images serve as a place to collect and hold together facts to be remembered. By including names, dates, and places in their images, students can remember a substantial collection of information. For example, visualization is a useful technique for remembering clusters of information, such as the names of the bones in the body, geographical features of a landscape, or parts of an automobile engine.

Tell students this activity will help them learn how to visualize to remember information. Answer any questions they may have about the technique. Have students read the paragraph on "Indoor Air Pollution" and complete the activity.

## 1-3   Using Categorization to Remember Information

Categorization involves organizing information in a way that makes it easier to remember. For example, the categories *flowers* and *foods* can be used to remember this set of words: *milk, rose, violet, meat, bread, orchid.* It is easier to remember two sets of three related words than one set of six words that may or may not be related.

Use the first part of the activity to help students understand the value of categorization as an aid to remembering information. Then have students complete the activity.

## 1-4   Using Application to Remember Information

Application involves doing something to remember information. For example, creating a miniature stage set for a Shakespearean play will help students recall the characters, setting, plot, events, and ending. Similarly, when students use a math formula to determine how large a desk they can fit into their study place, they are using application to remember the formula for area.

Explain how application can be used to remember information. Review the different ways of applying information to remember information. Ask students if they can add other forms of application to the list provided. Add any you think are valuable. Assign letters to these and have students add them to the list. Then have students complete the activity.

### 1-5  Using Repetition to Remember Information

Repetition involves repeatedly saying, looking at, and writing information to be remembered. For example, repetition is a common technique used by students to remember how to spell a word by saying, looking at, and writing the word several times.

Explain the repetition procedure. Tell students that they will practice using repetition to remember the meaning of new words. Then have students complete the activity. You can extend the activity by adding words from the subjects you are teaching.

### 1-6  Using Rhyme to Remember Information

The use of rhyme is a simple yet powerful technique for remembering information, often taught to students in songs and verses. Introduce these as examples of rhymes used to remember information:

> In fourteen hundred ninety-two,
> Columbus sailed the ocean blue.
>
> Thirty days hath September,
> April, June, and November.

Ask students to provide examples of rhymes they have used to remember information. Use the Shakespeare rhyme on the reproducible page to demonstrate the technique. Add any other examples you can think of that relate to what you are teaching. Then have students complete the activity. Finally, have students read aloud some of the rhymes they have created.

### 1-7  Using Acronyms to Remember Information

An acronym is a word created from the first letter of other words that are to be remembered. The computer terms RAM and ROM are acronyms for Random Access Memory and Read Only Memory. An acronym does not have to be a real word, but it must be a word that can be pronounced. The acronym NATO stands for North Atlantic Treaty Organization. Although NATO is not a real word, it can be pronounced.

Explain what an acronym is and review the procedure for forming acronyms. Then have students complete the page.

### 1-8  Using Abbreviations to Remember Information

Like acronyms, abbreviations are formed using the first letter of each word to be remembered. Abbreviations differ in that they do not form a pronounceable word. Common examples of abbreviations include IBM, NFL, and FBI.

Bring out the difference between abbreviations and acronyms. Then have students complete the page.

### 1-9  Using Acronymic Sentences to Remember Information

When using this remembering technique, students create sentences made up of words that begin with the initial letter of each of the items to be remembered. A common example used to remember the order of planets in our solar system is the acronymic sentence: *My* (Mercury) *very* (Venus) *earthy* (Earth) *mother* (Mars) *just* (Jupiter) *served* (Saturn) *us* (Uranus) *nine* (Neptune) *pizzas* (Pluto). Acronymic sentences are particularly useful when an acronym cannot be formed or when facts have to be remembered in a specific order.

Bring out that acronymic sentences are useful to remember information for which it is difficult to form an acronym. Use the example provided for the order of the planets to demonstrate how students can form an acronymic sentence. Then have students complete the activity.

### 1-10  Using Pegwords to Remember Information

Pegwords are rhyming words used to remember information in a certain order. To use this technique, students must first memorize a set of rhyming words for the numbers 1 through 10. We suggest these words. You can substitute other words.

| Number Word | Pegword |
| --- | --- |
| one | run |
| two | shoe |
| three | tree |
| four | door |
| five | hive |
| six | sticks |
| seven | heaven |
| eight | gate |
| nine | vine |
| ten | hen |

Once students have memorized the pegword for each number, they can use these pegwords to remember information. This is done by forming a mental image linking the pegword with the information to be remembered.

For example, pegwords can be used to remember the ten rights guaranteed under the Bill of Rights. The first right is freedom of religion, and the first pegword is *run*. To remember this first right, a student might form a mental image of people running from a church as they are chased by soldiers.

Present the pegwords for 1 through 10. Have students use repetition until they have automatic recall of the pegwords. Once students have achieved automatic recall, use the example of the first two rights from the Bill of Rights to demonstrate how pegwords can be used to remember information in order. Then have students use pegwords to remember the remaining rights.

### 1-11 Using Keywords to Remember Information

The keyword technique is useful for remembering the meaning of new and difficult vocabulary words or terms. Here are the three steps for using the keyword technique:

1. Students find a word that sounds like the word or part of the word to be learned. The acoustically similar word should be one that students already know and that is easy to picture. For example, for the word *reinforcer* (a reinforcer is anything that increases the probability that a person will do the same thing again) a student might substitute the keyword *force*.
2. Students use *force* to form a picture in their minds. The picture should illustrate the meaning of the word to be learned. For example, students might form a mental image of a coach forcing a player to shoot free throws over and over until 10 in a row are made.
3. To recall the definition of the new word, students recall the keyword and then its associated mental picture. Visualizing a player being forced to shoot free throws repeatedly will help students recall that a reinforcer is something that makes it likely that a person will do something again.

Bring out that using keywords is an excellent technique for remembering the meaning of difficult vocabulary words. Use the example provided for the vocabulary word *ellipse* to demonstrate the three steps. Then have students complete the activity. Incorporate new words from subjects you are teaching.

### 1-12 Remembering Information

The purpose of this activity is to have students apply what they have learned about remembering information. Have students identify information they need to remember. Then have students select techniques they would use to remember the information. Have students explain why they selected each technique.

### 1-13 Chapter One Mastery Assessment

Have students complete this assessment at any point at which you believe they have learned to use the remembering techniques presented in this chapter. Review the results of the assessment with the students. Provide additional instruction as necessary.

The human brain is not like a tape recorder that records everything that goes into it. Your brain does not remember everything your eyes, ears, and other senses bring to it. The brain remembers mostly what you select to remember. This is why the first step in the Remembering Strategy is to *select* what you need to remember.

Here is what you should do to select what you need to remember:

- Ask your teacher what is most important for you to remember.
- Examine your class notes and underline or use a highlight pen to mark the information you need to remember.
- Read the text assignments and take notes on the important information and ideas you need to remember.
- Examine your class handouts and underline or use a highlight pen to mark the information you need to remember.

Now think about a test one of your teachers will soon be giving you. Follow these steps to *select* the information you need to remember for the test.

1. Talk with your teacher about the test. In the space below, write the important information your teacher told you to remember for the test. Write the information here.

2. Look at your class notes. What information do you need to remember from your class notes for the test? Write the information here.

3. Examine the reading assignments that will be covered on the test. What information do you need to remember from your reading assignments for the test? Write the information here.

4. Review the class handouts that will be covered on the test. What information do you need to remember from these handouts? Write the information here.

Visualization means forming a picture in your mind. Visualization is a good way to remember things that are easy to picture. Sometimes you can create one or more pictures as you are reading. Other times you will need to reread the text to do this.

Read the following selection and try to create one or more pictures as you do so. If you cannot create pictures as you are reading, create them during a rereading of the selection.

### Indoor Air Pollution

There are three parts to the problem of indoor air pollution in today's world. First, increasing numbers and types of products and equipment used in homes, factories and offices give off fumes that may be dangerous. Second, buildings are so well insulated that pollutants are trapped inside and often build to dangerous levels. Third, people spend 90 percent of their time indoors. The people who spend the most time indoors are young children, old people, pregnant women, and people who are sick. These are the people who are the most likely to be harmed by pollutants. Many things that are commonly used may produce pollution. These things include: no-iron sheets and pillowcases, automobiles, by-products of foods cooked on the stove or in the oven, furnaces and heaters, glues and hobby materials, air fresheners, and aerosol sprays. Smoking is another major source of air pollution.

Now cover the selection and recall your pictures. Write what you see.

Finally, compare what you wrote with the information in the selection. Did you leave out any important information? What?

Sometimes you have to remember in your mind lists of words or details. Suppose you had to buy the following nine items at the supermarket: orange juice, lettuce, white bread, cucumbers, soda, English muffins, milk, dinner rolls, onions. You have a better chance of remembering the items if you organize them into categories.

| *Baked Goods* | *Liquids* | *Vegetables* |
|---|---|---|
| white bread | orange juice | lettuce |
| English muffins | soda | cucumbers |
| dinner rolls | milk | onions |

As you recall a category, you will also recall the items in it. In this example, it is easier to remember sets of three related things than to remember a set of nine things that are not all related. When you organize items to be remembered into categories, you are using a technique called **categorization.**

Now form categories to help you remember the following sources of pollution in the environment: ovens, automobiles, liquid detergent, stoves, trucks, bleach, furniture polish, airplanes, gas barbecues. Write the name of each category. Under each category name write the sources of pollution that belong to that category.

How did categorization help you remember the sources of pollution?

Can you think of another set of information for which categorization would be helpful?

# Using Application to Remember Information

When you try to remember information by using it in some way, you are using a technique called **application.**

Here are some ways you can use application to remember information:

a. Plan a trip.
b. Write a story.
c. Create a game.
d. Act out a role.
e. Cook a meal from a recipe.
f. Collect examples of things.
g. Collect or take photographs.
h. Create a rule that explains.

i. Prepare a time line.
j. Write a newspaper article.
k. Draw a picture.
l. Write and give a speech.
m. Draw a map.
n. Develop a formula.
o. Create a diorama.
p. Build a model.

Now write the letter that shows the application you would use to remember each of the following:

1. _____ The names of presidents of the United States since 1972

2. _____ The names of the states that border Mexico

3. _____ How to get from one place to another

4. _____ The states of matter in the universe

5. _____ The ingredients of a recipe

6. _____ The names of the starting players on your school's basketball team

7. _____ The events leading to the Persian Gulf War

8. _____ The parts of a home computer

9. _____ The formula for sodium chloride

10. _____ The names of five types of cats

# Using Repetition to Remember Information

When you read, say, and write information a number of times to remember it, you are using **repetition.** Here is how repetition is done:

### Repetition Procedure
1. Read the information aloud.
2. Close your eyes and repeat the information.
3. Write the information from memory.
4. Repeat the steps at least three times or until you can remember the information without error.

Follow the steps in the repetition procedure to remember the meanings of these words:

**mitosis**      Cell division resulting in two new cells.

**veto**      Turn down a bill or law.

**satellite**      An object that orbits another object.

**conquest**      Act of winning by war.

**epoch**      Smallest subdivision on the geologic time scale.

**neutral**      Not taking sides.

You can use rhymes to remember information. Here are two helpful rhymes.

> In fourteen hundred ninety two,
> Columbus sailed the ocean blue.

> Thirty days hath September
> April, June, and November.

You do not have to be a poet to make rhymes. Let your imagination run wild. If you can create a rhyme that works for you, use it. If you cannot make a rhyme, use one of the other remembering techniques.

Here is a rhyme for remembering who wrote *King Lear.*

> Do you know a play by Shakespeare?
> Absolutely, he wrote King Lear.

Create a rhyme for each of the following. Whenever you can't, write NO CAN RHYME!

1. Thomas Edison invented the electric light bulb.

2. Lansing is the capital of Michigan.

3. There are 360 degrees in a circle.

4. Jefferson was president of the United States when the Louisiana Purchase was made.

5. China has the largest population in the world.

6. The Ice Age ended 10,000 years ago.

7. Objects that have like electric charges repel each other.

8. A literacy test is a test to determine if a person can read and write.

9. A black hole is matter so dense that not even light can escape its gravity.

An **acronym** is a word made from the first letter of a set of words or terms that are to be remembered. Some acronyms are real words. Other acronyms are not real words, but they are words that can easily be pronounced. Small words like **for, the,** and **a** usually are not included in the acronym, but small words can be used when needed to create an acronym that can be pronounced. ROM is an example of an acronym. In this acronym, R stands for Read, O for Only, and M for Memory. ROM will help you to remember the meaning of this important computer term.

Write the commonly used acronym for each of the following:

1. Organization of Petroleum Exporting Countries

2. Mothers Against Drunk Drivers

3. North Atlantic Treaty Organization

4. Special Weapons Action Team

5. National Organization for Women

Write what these common acronyms stand for:

6. SALT

7. AWOL

8. AIDS

9. HUD

10. NASA

Now see if you can form acronyms for information you might find in your social studies and science textbooks. For example, here is an acronym that can help you to remember the names of the five Great Lakes: HOMES.

In this acronym, H stands for Lake Huron, O for Lake Ontario, M for Lake Michigan, E for Lake Erie, and S for Lake Superior.

Because the Great Lakes do not have to be remembered in a certain order, the lakes were arranged into an order that produced a word. Many times you will have to remember words or terms in a certain order. Because you will not be able to rearrange the words or terms to be remembered, it will be harder to form an acronym. In these cases you might want to use abbreviations or acronymic sentences. Both of these techniques for remembering information are taught later in this chapter.

Write an acronym for each of the following:

11. Native American tribes: Comanche, Sioux, Apache, Pequot

12. Elements: lithium, phosphorous, aluminum, radium, oxygen

# Using Abbreviations to Remember Information

Like acronyms, **abbreviations** use the first letters of words to be remembered. The difference between acronyms and abbreviations is that you do not have to be able to pronounce an abbreviation. Instead, you simply recite the letters in order. Small words **for, the,** and **a** should be left out when you form an abbreviation.

For example, the National Football League can be remembered as the abbreviation NFL, where N stands for National, F stands for Football, and L stands for League. You only have so much room in your memory. Three letters take up far less room than three words. Imagine how much room you will save in your memory if you use many abbreviations. You can use the room you save to remember other important information.

Form the commonly used abbreviation for each of the following:

1. National Broadcasting Company

2. District of Columbia

3. Unidentified flying object

4. Internal Revenue Service

5. Doctor of Dental Surgery

Write what these common abbreviations stand for:

6. TGIF

7. DJ

8. BMOC

9. IBM

10. CPA

Now see if you can form abbreviations for information you might find in your social studies and science textbooks. For example, you can use the abbreviation **UCM** to stand for **uniform circular motion.** Of course, you will still need to know that uniform circular motion refers to motion with constant speed around a circle.

Write an abbreviation for each of the following:

11. Confederate States of America

12. Periodic Table of the Elements

# Using Acronymic Sentences to Remember Information

**Acronymic sentences** are useful when you have to remember information for which you cannot form an acronym. You can form an acronymic sentence by using words that begin with the first letters of the items you wish to remember. For example, you can remember the order of the planets in our solar system according to their position from the sun by using the acronymic sentence "My (Mercury) very (Venus) earthy (Earth) mother (Mars) just (Jupiter) served (Saturn) us (Uranus) nine (Neptune) pizzas (Pluto)."

Create acronymic sentences for the information that follows. In some cases you will have to remember the information in order. In other cases you can rearrange the information to make it easier to create an acronymic sentence.

1. The first four hydrocarbons of the alkaline class: methane, ethane, propane, butane

2. The countries that make up Central America: Guatemala, Honduras, Nicaragua, Costa Rica, Panama, El Salvador, Belize

3. Five major rivers found in the United States: Pearl, Cumberland, Hudson, Platte, Rio Grande

4. Substances obtained from petroleum: gasoline, kerosene, lubricants, paraffins, asphalt

5. The first five presidents of the United States: George Washington, John Adams, Thomas Jefferson, James Madison, James Monroe

6. Geologic time periods in order from oldest to most recent: Precambrian, Paleozoic, Mesozoic, Cenozoic

**Pegwords** are words that rhyme with the number words **one** through **ten**. The number words helps you remember the pegwords. For example, the number **one** will help you recall its pegword **run.** Here are pegwords for the number words **one** through **ten.**

| Number Word | Pegword |
|---|---|
| one | run |
| two | shoe |
| three | bee |
| four | door |
| five | hive |
| six | sticks |
| seven | heaven |
| eight | gate |
| nine | vine |
| ten | hen |

Here is an example of how pegwords can be used to remember the ten rights granted under the Bill of Rights. The first is "freedom of religion." Form a mental picture that links *run* (the pegword for *one*) with freedom of religion. You could create a picture of a group of people *running* out of a church being chased by soldiers with guns. This picture will remind you that the first right under the Bill of Rights is "freedom of religion." To remember this, think of the word *run.* The word *run* will bring back into mind the picture of people running from a church being chased by soldiers. The second right is that "states can have a national guard." You can remember this by using the pegword *shoe* to form a picture of an armed soldier guarding a giant shoe.

You can use the remaining pegwords to remember the other rights guaranteed under the Bill of Rights.

| | |
|---|---|
| *three/bee* | We don't have to give food or shelter to soldiers during peacetime. |
| *four/door* | Our homes can't be searched without a search warrant signed by a judge. |
| *five/hive* | A person can't be brought to trial without evidence. |
| *six/sticks* | A person accused of a crime has the right to a speedy trial. |
| *seven/heaven* | You have a right to a trial by a jury of your peers. |
| *eight/gate* | Punishment for a crime must not be excessive. |
| *nine/vine* | Workers have the right to strike. |
| *ten/hen* | States run the public schools. |

You can use **keywords** to remember the meaning of new and difficult vocabulary words you read in your textbooks or hear in class. There are three things to do when you use keywords:

1. Change the word whose meaning you need to remember into a keyword whose meaning you already know. Your keyword should sound like the new word or a major part of the new word. Also, it should be a word that you can easily change into a mind picture and that sounds like the word to be learned. For example, you might substitute the familiar word *lips* for the new vocabulary word *ellipse*.

2. Form a picture in your mind that relates your keyword to the new or unfamiliar word. The word *ellipse* means a flattened circle. In this example, you might form a picture in your mind of someone leaning toward you to kiss you whose lips are shaped like a flattened circle. Sometimes you may need to form a series of mental pictures.

3. You must use your picture(s) to help you retrieve the meaning of the new word. Think of your keyword for the word whose meaning you wish to remember, and then recall what was happening in the picture you formed in your mind. In the example given, picturing someone about to kiss you whose lips are shaped like a flattened circle will help you to remember that an ellipse is a flattened circle.

Now practice using the keyword technique to remember the meaning of the words that follow. The meaning for each word is provided. If you need to, use the pronunciation key from a dictionary to pronounce the word. For each word, write your keyword and then describe the picture(s) you formed in your mind.

**New Word** **catalyst:** a substance that changes the rate of a chemical reaction without any change to its own structure

      Write your keyword:
      Describe your picture(s):

**New Word** **megalopolis:** a heavily populated area including several large cites and their suburbs

      Write your keyword:
      Describe your picture(s):

**Select** and write the information you need to remember for a test.

List the **techniques** you would use to remember the information. Explain why you selected each technique.

See what you have learned about remembering information:

1.  What are four things to do to select important information to remember?

2.  What is **visualization?**

3.  How does **categorization** help you remember information?

4.  What is remembering information by using it called?

5.  Write the four steps in the **repetition** procedure.

6.  Do you need to be a poet to create rhymes?

7.  What is an **acronym?**

8.  How is an abbreviation different?

9.  When would you form an **acronymic sentence?**

10. What are **pegwords?**

11. Write three things to do you when using **keywords.**

**1-1** Responses will vary depending on the test selected by each student.

**1-2** Responses will vary according to the mental picture formed by each student.

**1-3**

| *Means of Transportation* | *Household Cleaners* | *Cooking Devices* |
|---|---|---|
| automobiles | liquid detergent | ovens |
| trucks | bleach | stoves |
| airplanes | furniture polish | gas barbecue |

Other answers will vary.

**1-4** Best answers are: 1. i. 2. m. 3. a. 4. g. 5. e. 6. j. 7. b 8. p. 9. m. 10. c.

**1-5** Observe students as they use the repetition procedure.

**1-6** Answers will vary with students' creativity. For example, for item 1, a possible rhyme is:

At night when I have to take my medicine
I switch on the light bulb invented by Edison.

Or, for item 2,

When in Michigan and I want to go dancing,
I'll go to its capital, Lansing.

**1-7** 1. OPEC. 2. MADD. 3. NATO. 4. SWAT. 5. NOW 6. Strategic Arms Limitation Treaty. 7. Absent Without Leave. 8. Acquired Immune Deficiency Syndrome. 9. Housing and Urban Development. 10. National Aeronautics and Space Administration. 11. CAPS. 12. POLAR.

**1-8** 1. NBC. 2. DC. 3. UFO. 4. IRS 5. DDS. 6. Thank God It's Friday. 7. Disk Jockey. 8. Big Man On Campus. 9. International Business Machines. 10. Certified Public Accountant. 11. CSA. 12. PTE.

**1-9** Answers will vary with students' creativity. For example, for item 1, a possible acronymic sentence is: *Mary eats peanut butter.* Or, for item 2, *Harry got every new coin before paying.*

**1-10** Answers will vary with students' creativity. For example, for item 1, a possible mental picture retrieved using the pegword *run* might include two runners in a race. One runner is wearing a jersey with Articles of Confederation across the front. The second runner's jersey shows the words Continental Congress. The second runner has just passed the first. The second image retrieved using the pegword *shoe* might show a map of the 13 original states with shoe prints on each state. Similar images would be created for the remaining rights.

**1-11** Answers will vary with students' creativity. For example, for *catalyst*, the acoustic word could be *cat.* The mental images formed could begin by showing a lab technician slowly pouring two different-colored chemicals into a beaker. Then a cat jumps up and knocks against the technician's arm, causing the technician to pour the chemicals more quickly. The two chemicals pour into the beaker, producing a new color, and the cat runs off. These mental images help the student recall that a catalyst brings about an increase in the rate of chemical change without changing the catalyst. Similarly, mental images can be formed to remember the meaning of the word *megalopolis.*

**1-12** Students' responses will vary.

**1-13**
1. Ask the teacher; examine class notes; read assignments; examine handouts.
2. Forming a picture in your mind of something you need to remember.
3. Organizes the information to be remembered.
4. Application.
5. Read the information aloud, close eyes and repeat the information, write the information from memory, repeat first three steps until the information is remembered.
6. No.
7. A word made up from the first letter of each of a set of words to be remembered.
8. Does not have to pronounceable.
9. When information has to be remembered in a certain order and it is hard to create an acronym.
10. Words that rhyme with number words and can be used to remember information.
11. Change the word to be remembered into a word you know that sounds like the word to be remembered; form an image in your mind that relates the keyword to the word to be remembered; use the image to retrieve the meaning of the word to be remembered.

## CHAPTER TWO

# Reading and Taking Notes from Textbooks

## CHAPTER OBJECTIVES

1. Teach students to use the SQ3R textbook reading and notetaking strategy.
2. Teach students to apply SQ3R to reading assignments in their textbooks.

## TITLES OF REPRODUCIBLE ACTIVITIES

2-1 Introducing SQ3R
2-2 Survey, Question, Read
2-3 Reading Assignment: A Visit to Ancient Rome
2-4 Question–Answer Notetaking Form: A Visit to Ancient Rome
2-5 Recite and Review
2-6 Reading Assignment: Improving Muscular Strength and Endurance
2-7 Question–Answer Notetaking Form: Improving Muscular Strength and Endurance
2-8 Reading Assignment: Nature of Communication
2-9 Question–Answer Notetaking Form: Nature of Communication
2-10 Applying SQ3R: Question–Answer Notetaking Form
2-11 Chapter Two Mastery Assessment

## USING THE REPRODUCIBLE ACTIVITIES

After you have distributed a reproducible activity here are suggestions for its use. Feel free to add further information, illustrations or examples.

### 2-1 Introducing SQ3R*

The formula SQ3R stands for the five steps of this textbook reading and notetaking strategy: Survey, Question, Read, Recite, and Review. The first three steps, Survey, Question, and Read, are used by the reader to comprehend the textual information. The last two steps, Recite and Review, are used to help the reader retain the information.

The purpose of the Survey step is to activate the prior knowledge of the reader and to familiarize the reader with the content of the reading selection. Here is what the student must do:

- Read the title and think about what it means.
- Read the introduction, which is usually found in the first paragraph or two.
- Read the side headings to learn what the selection is about.
- Examine all the visuals and read their captions.
- Read the conclusion, which is usually found in the last paragraph or two.

The purpose of the Question step is to provide the reader with questions to think about and answer while reading. These questions force the reader to interact with the author to locate information that will answer the questions. While reading to answer questions, the reader remains active in the reading process. Students who read without a clear purpose in mind frequently become inactive readers. Their eyes move across lines and from page to page while their minds record nothing.

Questions are formed by placing the words *who, what, where, when, why,* or *how* in front of the title to form one or more questions about the title. Each side heading is changed into one or more questions by following the same procedure. More than one question should be written for a title or side heading if a single question would be too complex.

In many cases teachers will assign parts of chapters to be read. In these cases there may be no title. When this occurs, the students should be instructed to proceed by writing questions for side headings only.

The purpose of the Read step is for the reader to get the information needed to answer the questions formed in the previous step. Students should be encouraged to skim, skip, read, and/or reread material as appropriate to answer each question. They should write the answers to each question on the form shown in Reproducible Activity 2-4. It is not necessary for students to write answers in complete sentences. Students should be encouraged to use abbreviations and to write answers with as few words as possible. The written answers to the questions then become textbook notes, which students can use to review the chapter information and prepare for tests.

Students should be told that sometimes while reading they will discover that a question they formed does not match the information presented by the author. When this is the case, students should be directed to change their question to match the information presented.

The purpose of the Recite step is for students to fix the information in their short-term memory. Immediately after textbook notes have been completed, for each question students should:

- Read the question and its answer aloud.
- Read the question aloud, then look away and say the answer aloud.
- Read the question aloud, then with eyes closed say the answer aloud.
- Repeat this procedure three times.

The purpose of the Review step is for the reader to fix the information in long-term memory. The same procedure used in the Recite step is followed. The difference is that the recitation is done over a number of days to fix the questions and answers in long-term memory. Students will vary in the number of times and days needed for review. Students with memory difficulties will have to review more often. We recommend that students review for at least three days.

Review with students the purposes and components of SQ3R. Then have students write the words that go with each letter in the diagram of SQ3R and answer the questions that follow.

### 2-2 Survey, Question, Read

Review the first three steps in SQ3R. Then have students complete the activity to decide what is most important to remember about each step.

### 2-3 Reading Assignment: A Visit to Ancient Rome

### 2-4 Question–Answer Notetaking Form

Have students survey "A Visit to Ancient Rome" on 2-3. Then have the students turn the title and side headings into questions they write on the Question-Answer Notetaking Form on 2-4. Finally have students read to answer their questions and write their answers on 2-4.

### 2-5 Recite and Review

Review the last two steps in SQ3R. Then have students complete the activity to decide what is most important to remember about each step. Then direct the students to apply the RR steps to their answers on 2-4.

### 2-6  Reading Assignment: Improving Muscular Strength and Endurance

### 2-7  Question–Answer Notetaking Form

Have students survey "Improving Muscular Strength and Endurance" on 2-6. Then have the students turn the title and side headings into questions they write on the Question–Answer Notetaking Form on 2-7. Point out that the names of the title and side headings are not provided and need not be written on this form. Finally, have students read to answer their questions and write their answers on 2-7.

### 2-8  Reading Assignment: Nature of Communication

### 2-9  Question–Answer Notetaking Form

Have students survey "Nature of Communication" on 2-8. Then have the students turn the title and side headings into questions they write on the Question–Answer Notetaking Form on 2-9. Finally, have students read to answer their questions and write their answers on 2-9.

### 2-10  Applying SQ3R: Question–Answer Notetaking Form

This is the form students should be encouraged to use for each reading assignment. Give the students a reading assignment, have them apply SQ3R, and use 2-10 to write their questions and answers. Finally, have the students do the recite and review steps.

### 2-11  Chapter Two Mastery Assessment

Have students complete this assessment at any point you believe they have learned to use SQ3R. Review the results of the assessment with the students. Provide additional instruction as necessary.

**SQ3R** is a textbook reading and notetaking strategy that stands for <u>S</u>urvey, <u>Q</u>uestion, <u>R</u>ead, <u>R</u>ecite, and <u>R</u>eview.

The <u>S</u>urvey, <u>Q</u>uestion, and <u>R</u>ead components help you **understand** the information you read about in your textbooks. This is done by having you create questions and write answers to the questions as you read.

The <u>R</u>ecite and <u>R</u>eview components help you **remember** the information you have read about in your textbooks. This is done by reviewing and reciting the questions and answers.

Here is a diagram of the steps in SQ3R. Write the word that goes with each letter. Then answer the questions.

_____ S

_____ Q      Promotes Understanding

_____ R


_____ R
                        Promotes Remembering
_____ R

1. What do the Survey, Question, and Read components help you do?




2. What do the Recite and Review components help you do?




3. What combination of letters and a number helps you remember this textbook reading and notetaking strategy?

Here are the first three steps in the SQ3R strategy. Read to learn what you must do for each step in the strategy. Underline the words in each bulleted statement that will help you remember what to do.

S
Q  =  Understanding
R

**Survey** to become familiar with the content of your textbook reading assignment.

- Read the title and think about what it means.

- Read the introduction, which is usually found in the first paragraph or two.

- Read the side headings to learn what the selection is about.

- Examine all the visuals and read their captions.

- Read the conclusion, which is usually found in the last paragraph or two.

**Question** to provide purposes for reading.

- Change the title into one or more questions using the words *who, what, where, when, why,* and/or *how.* Write the question(s).

- Change each side heading into one or more questions using the words *who, what, where, when, why,* and/or *how.* Write the question(s).

- Also write questions your teacher tells you to answer.

**Read** to get the information needed to answer the questions.

- Sometimes a question you write cannot be answered from the information in the textbook. When this occurs, change the question to match the information presented.

- Write answers to questions to form textbook notes.

- Create a graphic organizer to show how the information in your notes can be organized.

- Recall the remembering strategies you learned in Chapter One. Select one or more to help you remember the information in your notes.

# Reading Assignment: A Visit to Ancient Rome

**2-3**

To apply SQR to part of a textbook chapter about Ancient Rome, do the following:

1. Survey the chapter.
2. Change the title and side headings into questions. Write the questions on the Question–Answer Notetaking Form provided in Activity 2-4.
3. Read to find the answers to your questions. Write the answers on the Question–Answer Notetaking Form.

---

## A Visit to Ancient Rome

What do you think living in Rome was like a thousand or more years ago? It was quite exciting for he times because Rome was the cultural center of the known world. By taking a visit to ancient Rome, you will obtain a feeling for this marvelous city.

### Roman Dress

The first thing a traveler to ancient Rome would see would be some male citizens going about their daily business dressed in long, woolen shirts called tunics. Those men who were involved in more formal routines would be wearing undyed wool togas over their tunics. In most weather all Romans wore strap sandals. The ladies of the city dressed in long stolas, tunics belted at the waist, worn over an inner tunic. They might wear a rectangular cloak if the weather was cold. Roman women often carried parasols and fans in hot weather. All the citizens dressed as comfortably as they could.

### Forms of Entertainment

As he toured the city, the newcomer might wonder what forms of entertainment amused the citizens. He would probably hear shouts and cheers coming from an area where spectators were enjoying a circus, a play, or gladiatorial combat. These events took place often and lasted from sunrise to sundown. Admission was free so anyone who chose to could attend.

Another popular leisure time activity in ancient Rome was public bathing. Bathing establishments were quite elaborate. One would find games, lectures, and musical performances presented there. There were areas where people could lounge and gossip if they were not enjoying the baths. At the center of everything were the baths themselves, a cold bath, a warm bath, and a steam bath which bathers passed through in order. The baths were actually a large complex of business and entertainment areas.

---

**28**

## Limitations of the City

The tourist would be impressed with the Roman's love of grandeur as evidenced by the beauty of baths, but if he walked around the city long enough, he would become aware of the limitations it had. It would soon be obvious that as a visitor he would have to ask directions in order to get around. Most of the residential streets did not have names and the houses did not have numbers. There were few sidewalks and the streets were narrow and crowded. The tourist would have to be alert when he strolled down a residential street because at that time people disposed of their trash the easiest way, by throwing it out the window! Thus, walking around Rome was not only confusing, it was also dangerous.

## Rome at Night

Anyone visiting Rome would be well advised to do his sightseeing during the day because a walk through Rome at night was a dangerous adventure. There were no street lights to illuminate the heavy traffic that clogged the streets. During the day law prohibited chariots and tradesmen's carts from filling the streets of the city, so there was a great deal of traffic at night. There was also a lot of crime in the dark, crowded streets. Smart Romans stayed at home after sunset.

## Hazards of Travel

When the visitor to Rome decided to leave, he would have to choose his route home carefully. Travel outside the city was dangerous and difficult. Wealthy people traveled by carriage, usually accompanied by their household slaves and servants. Travelers would not stop at the inns and hotels along the way because they were apt to be dirty. They also tended to be the hangouts of robbers. Instead the Roman traveler would sleep in his carriage or in a tent put up by the side of the road. If the traveler was fortunate and had a friend who lived along the route, he could stay with him. There was an elaborate social system of *hospitium* or "guest friendship" that was similar to membership in a lodge. People were obligated to give those who were their friends protection and hospitality while they were on the road. Romans had to plan their journey well if they were to arrive at their destination safely.

You can see that living in the ancient city of Rome was both adventurous and dangerous. Life was very different from what we experience in the twentieth century. Dress, entertainment, travel, and conditions of living are much better today.

102   LIVING LONG AGO

# Question–Answer Notetaking Form: A Visit to Ancient Rome

**2-4**

Use this form to write Questions and Answers for "A Visit to Ancient Rome."

1. Title: **"A Visit to Ancient Rome"**
   Question


   Answer


2. Side heading: Roman Dress
   Question


   Answer


3. Side heading: Forms of Entertainment
   Question


   Answer


4. Side heading: Limitations of the City
   Question


   Answer


4. Side heading: Rome at Night
   Question


   Answer


5. Side heading: Hazards of Travel
   Question


   Answer

**30**

Here are the final two steps in the SQ3R strategy. Read to learn what you must do for each step in the strategy. Underline the words in each bulleted statement that will help you remember what to do.

R
   = Remembering
R

**Recite** the information to keep it in your memory.

- Read each question and its answer aloud.

- Read each question aloud, then look away and say its answer aloud.

- Read each question aloud, then with eyes closed say its answer aloud.

- Repeat this procedure three times for each question and answer.

**Review** the information to keep the information in your memory for a long time.

- Recite the questions and answers once each day for at least three days.

Now apply the Recite and Review steps to the questions and answers you wrote on the Question–Answer Notetaking Form on 2-4.

Apply SQ3R to the following section. Write your questions and answers on the Question-Answer Notetaking Form on 2-7.

---

Although muscular strength and endurance are closely related, it is important to differentiate between the two. Muscular strength is the amount of force or weight a muscle or group of muscles can exert for one repetition. It is generally measured by a single maximal contraction. The amount of weight you can bench press overhead one time, for example, measures the strength of the triceps muscle. You can measure the strength of other muscle groups the same way with specific tests. Muscular endurance is the capacity of a muscle group to complete an uninterrupted series of repetitions as often as possible with light weights. The total number of bench presses you can complete with one-half of your maximum weight on the barbell, for example, measures the endurance of the triceps and pectoralis muscles. Depending on the desired outcome, you can manipulate the training variables (choice of equipment and exercises, amount of resistance or weight, number of repetitions and sets, length of rest interval) to make your program strength- or endurance-oriented or a balance of both.

This chapter addresses the key factors involved in training for the development of strength and endurance, including importance, influencing factors, training principles and suggestions, specific exercises, equipment, girth control, and other related concerns to help design a program to meet your specific needs.

### The Importance of Strength and Endurance

The improvement of muscular strength and endurance will affect almost every phase of your life. Some of the benefits, such as the loss of body fat and improved self-concept, have been overlooked in the past because of overemphasis on adding muscle mass and improving performance. A closer look at the true value of strength and endurance training makes it clear that a sound program can help to improve both physical and mental health.

### The Management of Body Weight and Fat

Although strength training is generally associated with muscle weight gain and not with body weight and fat loss, it is a critical part of a total weight-control program. Unfortunately, although metabolism slows with age, the amount of calories (cal) we consume does not. As a result, body weight and fat increase and the amount of lean muscle mass decreases. From 25 to 50 years of age, basal metabolism slows by as much as 15 percent in some sedentary individuals. The typical

From *Physical Fitness and Wellness* by Jerrold S. Greenberg, George P. Dintiman, and Barbee Myers Oakes, copyright © 1995 by Allyn and Bacon, Boston. Used with permission.

60-year-old, for example, burns about 350 fewer daily calories at rest than he or she burned at age 25. This is equivalent to one pound of fat (3500 cal = 1 lb of fat) every ten days, 3 lb per month, 36 lb per year. As you can see, even small decreases in metabolism produce large increases in body weight and fat. A 5 percent slowing of metabolic rate, for example, can add 6 to 9 lbs of body fat in just one year depending on your weight and size at the time.

This slowing of resting metabolism is a direct result of the loss of lean muscle mass through inactivity, something that happens to everyone who is, or becomes, inactive regardless of age. Although it requires energy (cal) to maintain muscle tissue at rest, fat or adipose tissue is almost metabolically inert and requires very few calories to maintain. A comparison of two individuals identical in weight, one with ten pounds more muscle than the other, clearly shows that the resting metabolism is significantly higher in the more muscled individual. According to some experts, resting metabolism increases by approximately 30 to 50 cal daily for every pound of muscle weight added. In other words, you burn enough extra calories at rest to lose three to five lbs a year for every pound of muscle mass you add.

Regular strength and endurance training and aerobic exercise can prevent much of this undesirable change in metabolic rate. In fact, a well-conceived weight-training program that emphasizes muscle-weight gain will actually increase basal metabolism regardless of age. For both women and men, aerobic exercise followed by a half-hour strength-training session three to four times weekly, coupled with sound nutrition, is an ideal approach to weight control throughout life.

### Improved Appearance, Body Image, and Self-Concept

Muscular strength and endurance training can improve your physical appearance. By reducing your caloric intake, losing body fat and weight, improving muscle tone, and adding muscle weight, you will look better.

When weight loss occurs too rapidly, particularly without exercise, skin gives the appearance of not fitting the body very well. Sagging skin on the back of the arms, for example, is often an indication of either too rapid, or too large an amount of, weight loss. With reduced caloric intake, fat cells shrink but the skin does not keep pace to provide a tight fit. One way to improve appearance and help your skin fit better during and after weight loss is to include strength training as part of your total program. As fat cells shrink in the back of your arms, for example, strength training can enlarge the tricep muscle tissue to help avoid sagging skin.

Keep in mind that these changes will not occur overnight. Depending on age and current physical state, it may take 12 months or more of regular aerobic exercise, strength and endurance training, and dietary management of calories to decrease total body fat significantly, add 5 to 10 pounds of muscle weight, tone the entire body, give skin sufficient time to rebound to a tight fit, and adjust to the new body. These changes will alter the way you both perceive yourself and feel others perceive you. Practically everyone who stays with a program experiences improved body image and self-concept that positively affects their personal and professional lives. Patience is necessary, however; proper nutrition and exercise, rather than diets, are meant to be lifetime activities.

## Increased Bone-Mineral Content

Recent studies suggest that regular strength training aids in optimal bone development by improving bone-mineral content. The use of strength training in addition to weight-bearing exercise, such as walking, jogging, racket sports, and aerobic dance, may help women reach menopause with more bone-mineral mass, an important factor in the prevention, and delay, of osteoporosis.

## Increased Strength and Endurance for Work and Daily Activities

Each of the training programs discussed in this chapter will effectively increase both muscular strength and endurance in the relatively short period of 8 to 12 weeks. If you are, for example, in the process of moving or helping a friend to move, you will notice an improvement in your ability to lift furniture and other heavy objects without undue fatigue. Additional strength and endurance will also help you perform daily personal and work activities more efficiently and provide you with the extra strength needed to cope with unexpected emergencies in life.

## Improved Performance in Sports and Recreational Activities

Children and adults often lack strength and endurance in the upper body (arms and shoulders) and in the abdominal area. Many studies also show that most women are weak in the arms and shoulders because they think strength training will cause a loss of femininity, a totally unfounded fear. It is important to recognize that individualized, safe weight-training programs can be designed for both sexes at all ages and that these programs will improve muscular strength and endurance in the upper body, stomach, lower back, and other areas with little or no health risks or change in femininity. Increased upper-body and abdominal strength and endurance also helps to improve physical appearance and self-concept. Such a program helps children and young adults to engage in a wide variety of sports such as tumbling, gymnastics, baseball, basketball, field hockey, touch football, and soccer. You will also notice a difference when you perform an aerobic exercise or dance class, a conditioning class, or participate in your favorite recreational activity. The additional strength and endurance will delay fatigue and make free movement easier.

## Decreased Incidence of Sports and Work-Related Injuries

Improved strength in the musculature surrounding the joints helps prevent injuries to your muscles, tendons, and ligaments. With regular training, bones and connective tissue become stronger and more dense. These changes make you less vulnerable to muscle strain, sprains, contusions, and tears. Even low back pain may be prevented by an improved balance of strength and flexibility in the abdominal and back extensor muscles.

Strength training is also an important part of recovery following certain injuries. Return to normal range of motion and strength following soft-tissue injuries occurs more rapidly and completely with rehabilitative strength training.

## Summary

Strength and endurance training provides health-related benefits for people of all ages. Such training burns calories, adds muscle mass, prevents the slowing of metabolism with age, and is an important aspect of controlling body weight and body fat throughout life. Over a period of 6 to 12 months of this training, your general physical appearance, body image, and self-concept will improve. Strength training also aids in the development of the skeletal system and in improving bone mineral content. The added strength and endurance acquired also increases energy and productivity on the job and in recreational activities and reduces the incidence of sports- and work-related injuries. And finally, strength and endurance training plays a major role in the rehabilitation of soft-tissue injuries such as muscle strains, tears, contusions, and surgery.

Question

Answer

Question

Answer

Question

Answer

Question

Answer

Question

Answer

Question

Answer

Add whatever number of questions and answers are necessary for the assignment. Also add any questions your teacher asks you to answer.

Apply SQ3R to the following selection. Write your questions and answers on the Question–Answer Notetaking Form on 2-9.

The development of skill in communication can assist you in many different ways. You will improve more easily if you understand what communication is and how it works. You have been communicating all of your life, but the performance of any activity is usually insufficient to develop an adequate understanding of it. The more you know about what communication is, the better your chances for engaging in it effectively.

## A Definition of Communication

When people use the term communication, they generally have in mind some notion involving an exchange of messages. In fact, a good way of defining **communication** is as the purposeful production and transmission of a message by a person to one or more other persons. When those to whom our messages are directed receive, interpret, and act in accordance with our intentions, then we say that communication is successful. If messages are not received, interpreted, and acted upon in the ways we intend, we often use such expressions as *communication breakdown* and miscommunication to describe the situation. Much of this book is about how to avoid failures in communication. You can more easily avoid failure if you know how communication works.

## Objectives of Communication

Each of us has many different and specific reasons for engaging in communication. We communicate to "let off steam," make friends, obtain information about matters of personal importance, improve our positions in organizations, help others deal with their problems, pass time, change people's opinions, gain acceptance, create favorable impressions, and so on. Whatever compels us to communicate, once we are engaged in communication, we seek to accomplish something. This "something" is an **objective**, or the end toward which communicative activity is directed. This is what makes communication purposeful. All communication, in one way or another, is directed toward one or both of two ends: the creation of shared meanings and influence.

*Creation of Shared Meanings.* When we communicate, we often want others to understand a point, know what we are thinking, have a particular perception, or

From *Mastering Communication* (Second Edition) by Dennis S. Gouran, William E. Wiethoff, and Joel A. Doelger. Copyright © 1994 by Allyn and Bacon, Boston.

acquire new information. In each case, success is measured by the extent to which those with whom we communicate develop similar meanings for those objects, people, or events to which our messages refer (Littlejohn, 1992). In other words, we want others to be similar to us in how they view and comprehend the thoughts, ideas, and feelings we express (Gregg, 1984). When we achieve such similarity, we say that communication has "high fidelity." **Fidelity** is the correspondence between what a message producer has in mind and what a message recipient understands that person to have in mind.

Communication sometimes appears to be easier than we think. You may more fully appreciate the difficulty of communicating in a way that leads to shared meaning by trying the exercise in the following box. After completing the exercise, ask yourself the following questions: Did the person's picture come close to your description? What details were omitted? Were any details that you did not provide added? If you could repeat the exercise, how would you "change" your message to create closer correspondence between your mental image and the message recipient's reconstruction of it?

*Influence.*   In addition to creating shared meanings, we also frequently try to affect the recipients of our messages in other ways. Not only do we want them to understand what we think, feel, and believe; we also want them to accept our views, change their opinions, or behave in ways we think they should (Burgoon and Miller, 1990). When these are the ends toward which our communication is directed, the objective is to influence. As you will discover, the exercise of influence often requires approaches to communication that are different from those we follow when our objective is to create shared meanings. Influence is facilitated, however, by the successful creation of shared meanings (Bettinghaus and Cody, 1987).

## How Communication Works

For communication as we have defined it to take place, certain things must happen. You can think of communication as a series of events that occur in sequence. The sequence usually unfolds in eight stages: stimulation, motivation, generation, formation, transmission, reception, interpretation, and reaction.

*Stimulation.*   Communication arises in response to something that arouses us physically or psychologically. It may be another person, the sight of something unusual, a feeling of hunger, or any number of other states that we experience. **Stimulation** refers to any type of sensory or mental experience of which we become aware. The source of stimulation, whatever it might be, captures our attention. Not every experience, of course, leads to communication, but unless we are aroused in some way, communication will not occur. Without stimulation, we have nothing to communicate about.

*Motivation.*   Once a person is aroused—that is, experiences some sort of stimulation—often he or she will feel a need to respond. This feeling gives us a motive or reason to say something by some means. **Motivation** is a psychological condition that sets the direction for one's behavior. For instance, if someone angers you, you may be motivated to let the person know how you feel.

---

**Testing Your Communication Skill**

Think of some object that you consider easy to describe and that would not require much artistic skill to draw if another person could see the object. The front of your home or your desk are examples. Then prepare a written description of the object—one that you think is fully adequate for someone else to visualize what you have in mind. Read the description to a friend twice, and then ask him or her to draw the object.

---

*Generation.*   When a person is motivated by whatever has contributed to a feeling of arousal, he or she will begin to generate a message. **Generation** is a set of mental operations by which a communicator thinks about what he or she is going to say, or wishes to say. In this stage, the communicator explores what an experience appears to call for in the way of a response. A roommate's blaring radio, for instance, may prompt a request to turn down the volume—or if the person has been particularly inconsiderate, a demand.

*Formation (Encoding).*   After a communicator has generated thoughts about what to say, he or she will begin to form, or encode, a message. **Encoding** is the translation of thoughts into words and other types of symbolic expression that enable others to understand what the sender of a message wants them to know, think, feel, believe, or do. This is a very important stage in communication. No matter how clear your thoughts may be to you, if you cannot represent them in ways that those to whom your messages are directed can interpret accurately, you will have little success.

*Transmission.*   **Transmission** is the process by which a message is conveyed from the sender to the person or persons for whom it is intended. We transmit messages by various means. **Medium** is the term we use for a particular means of communication. Voice is a medium by which we convey a great many of our messages. We also use writing, sound, and visual images as media. Increasingly, we have come to rely on electronic means for transmitting messages. Whatever the medium, if the messages we send to not "arrive," there can be no communication.

*Reception.*   Up to this point, we have been talking about communication largely in terms of the message producer. Once communication has passed the transmission stage, however, those to whom a message is directed become the focus of concern. **Reception** occurs when an individual is aware of a message and recognizes it as such. The last part of this definition is very important. Not everything we become aware of is a message (King, 1988). When you hear the rain falling outside your window, you do not think of it as a message. Nor would most of us consider the sight of a speeding car as a message, even though we might react to it. In speaking of communication, then, we are concerned with only those situations in which one becomes aware of something that he or she recognizes as a message.

*Interpretation (Decoding).*    Since messages are representations of the sender's thoughts, reception alone is not sufficient for completion of the process of communication. If you received the message @%+#*)*!, it probably would not mean anything to you, even if the source of the message had something very important in mind to say to you. For this message to make sense, you would have to have some basis for knowing what the characters represent as thoughts. In short, you would have to be able to interpret, or decode, them. **Decoding** is a mental process by which one assigns meanings to messages and determines what the message producer presumably intends to say.

*Reaction.*    After the recipient interprets the message, he or she typically reacts in some way. **Reaction** refers to what an individual understands, believes, feels, or does as a result of his or her interpretation of a message. Usually, the recipient has more than one reaction. For instance, after listening to a persuasive speech on environmental hazards, you may (1) feel that you know much more about the issues addressed and (2) want to do something about the problem. Or, after listening to an acquaintance tell you about "what your problem is," you may (1) have hurt feelings, (2) change your attitude toward the person, and (3) say something in response that you later wish you had not. The reactions we have to messages are often the source of stimulation for forming our own messages, which we then transmit (either directly or indirectly) to the original message producer. We often refer to this type of message as feedback. **Feedback** is a special type of message revealing a person's reactions to what another person has said.

Because we do react to messages, at this stage, the process of communication begins anew. The message recipient becomes a message producer who generates, forms, and transmits new messages. The original message producer becomes a message recipient.

## Summary

Communication is the purposeful production and transmission of a message by a person to one or more other persons. The objectives of communication are to create shared meanings and to influence what others think, feel, believe, and do. There are several stages of communication: stimulation, motivation, generation, formation, transmission, reception, interpretation, and reaction. Message recipients reveal reactions by means of feedback. Feedback reverses the role of message producer and recipient, and thereby starts the process anew.

Question


Answer


Question


Answer


Question


Answer


Question


Answer


Question


Answer


Question


Answer


Add whatever number of Questions and Answers is necessary for the assignment. Also add any questions your teacher asks you to answer.

Book:                                                   Pages:        Date:

Question


Answer


Question


Answer


Question


Answer


Question


Answer


Question


Answer


Apply RR to remember these questions and answers.

Identify the step each letter stands for. Then explain what you should do for each step step.

S

Q

R

R

R

1. What do the steps SQR help you to accomplish?

2. What about RR?

**43**

**2-1** S = Survey, Q = Question, R = Read, R = Recite, R = Review.
1. Understand what I read. 2. Remember what I read. 3. SQ3R.

**2-2** Answers will vary.

**2-3** No writing required.

**2-4** Questions and Answers will vary.

**2-5** No writing required.

**2-6** No writing required.

**2-7** Questions and Answers will vary.

**2-8** No writing required.

**2-9** Questions and Answers will vary.

**2-10** Questions and Answers will vary.

**2-11** S = **Survey:** Read title, introduction, side headings, visuals, and conclusions.

Q = **Question:** Use the words **who, what, where, when, why,** or **how** to form questions from the title and side headings.

R = **Read:** Read to answer the questions.

R = **Recite:** Say the questions and answers aloud until they can be recalled.

R = **Review:** Do the same things as in the Recite step from time to time to make sure the information is remembered.
1. Understand what I read.
2. Remember what I read.

## CHAPTER THREE

# Taking Notes in Class

## CHAPTER OBJECTIVES

1. Teach students the three stages of notetaking.
2. Teach students to use abbreviations and symbols.
3. Teach students to identify lecture patterns.
4. Teach students to rewrite notes.

## TITLES OF REPRODUCIBLE ACTIVITIES

3-1 Notetaking Self-Assessment
3-2 What Did I Learn from My Self-Assessment?
3-3 Writing Less without Losing Meaning
3-4 Forming Abbreviations
3-5 Forming More Abbreviations
3-6 Using Symbols
3-7 How Lectures Are Organized: Topic–List
3-8 How Lectures Are Organized: Question–Answer
3-9 How Lectures Are Organized: Problem–Solution
3-10 How Lectures Are Organized: Cause–Effect
3-11 How Lectures Are Organized: Compare
3-12 How Lectures Are Organized: Contrast
3-13 Graphic Ways to Represent Your Notes
3-14 Reviewing the Notetaking Strategy
3-15 Two Techniques for Rewriting Notes
3-16 Practice Rewriting Notes
3-17 Chapter Three Mastery Assessment

## USING THE REPRODUCIBLE ACTIVITIES

After you have distributed a reproducible activity, here are suggestions for its use. Feel free to add further information, illustrations, or examples. Wherever possible, relate the activity to actual subject area assignments.

### 3-1  Notetaking Self-Assessment

Tell students that to take good notes in class they must do some things before they arrive at class, some things during class, and some things after class. Have students answer the questions to reveal what they do to get ready to take notes, how they take notes, and what they do with their notes.

### 3-2  What Did I Learn from My Self-Assessment?

Explain each step under Get Ready. Then have students check Yes or No to tell whether they included these steps in their responses to 3-1. Repeat this procedure for Take Notes and After Notes. If not raised by students, add general points such as skip between lines to allow room for editing, leave space between important ideas so that the ideas do not run together, write on one side of the page only, and ask questions when unsure of what was said by the teacher.

### 3-3  Writing Less without Losing Meaning

Use the introductory statement to discuss speaking and writing rates. Then have students answer the questions about the Mississippi River statement. Review the directions for writing less without losing meaning. Have students rewrite the Mississippi River statement and answer the questions.

### 3-4  Forming Abbreviations

Tell students they can increase their writing speed by using abbreviations. Use the examples to review common words and their standard abbreviations. Add others from materials you are using in your teaching. Point out to students that they can create their own abbreviations, but they must be able to recognize them later. Then have students complete the activity.

### 3-5  Forming More Abbreviations

Remind students of the purpose for using abbreviations and have them complete the activity.

### 3-6  Using Symbols

Tell students that another way to increase their writing speed is by using symbols. Review the examples provided. Add others from materials you are using in your teaching. Then have students complete the activity by rewriting the sentences in a shorter form using abbreviations and symbols.

### 3-7 How Lectures Are Organized: Topic–List

Tell students that teachers organize lectures in different ways. Use the introductory text to review the topic–list pattern. Then have students complete the activity.

### 3-8 How Lectures Are Organized: Question–Answer

Use the introductory text to review the question–answer lecture pattern. Then have students complete the activity.

### 3-9 How Lectures Are Organized: Problem–Solution

Use the introductory text to review the problem–solution lecture pattern. Then have students complete the activity.

### 3-10 How Lectures Are Organized: Cause–Effect

Use the introductory text to review the cause–effect lecture pattern. Then have students complete the activity.

### 3-11 How Lectures Are Organized: Compare

Use the introductory text to review the compare lecture pattern. Then have students complete the activity.

### 3-12 How Lectures Are Organized: Contrast

Use the introductory text to review the contrast lecture pattern. Then have students complete the activity.

### 3-13 Graphic Ways to Represent Your Notes

Review the graphic organizer for each lecture pattern. Emphasize that graphic organizers are used to show how ideas are related. Then have students share their experiences using graphic organizers.

### 3-14 Reviewing the Notetaking Strategy

Use this activity to demonstrate how graphic organizers can be used to show how ideas are related. For this activity, students will be using information from 3-2. After reviewing the example for Get Ready, have students complete the graphic organizer for Take Notes and After Notes.

### 3-15 Two Techniques for Rewriting Notes

Review both techniques for rewriting notes when rewriting is necessary. Have students tell which rewriting technique they prefer and explain why. Some may have a good reason for using both.

### 3-16 Practice Rewriting Notes

Have students rewrite their notes from 3-7 (Topic–List) using one or both techniques they learned in 3-14 and 3-15. Repeat for 3-8 (Question–Answer), 3-9 (Problem–Solution), 3-10 (Cause–Effect), 3-11 (Compare), and 3-12 (Contrast).

### 3-17 Chapter Three Mastery Assessment

Have students complete this assessment at any point you believe they have learned the notetaking skills presented in this chapter. Review the results of the assessment with the students. Provide additional instruction as necessary.

# Notetaking Self-Assessment

Think about how you take notes. Then answer these questions.

**1.** What things do you do to get ready to take notes in class? List them here.

**2.** What things do you do when you take notes in class? List them here.

**3.** What things do you do with your notes after class? List them here.

# What Did I Learn from My Self-Assessment?

Listen as your teacher explains each step in a strategy for taking notes. Check Yes or No before each statement to tell whether or not you included the idea in your Self-Assessment.

**Yes  No**

*Get Ready*
- Have notetaking materials ready.
- Review notes from previous day.
- Do assigned reading for that day's class.
- Predict the teacher's goal for that day's class.

*Take Notes*
- Listen for the teacher's statement of the goal.
- Use abbreviations and symbols.
- Listen for the teacher's lecture pattern.
- Write only the words needed to record the ideas presented.
- Copy information presented visually.
- Circle anything you wrote but did not understand.
- Underline unknown words and terms.
- Leave blanks for information missed.

*After Notes*
- Ask your teacher or other students to explain things in your notes you do not understand. Make the changes in your notes.
- Use the glossary or a dictionary to define unknown words and terms. Write the definitions in the margin.
- Compare your notes with those of other students to fill in any blanks. Go to the textbook or your teacher if you still need help.
- Rewrite your notes if they are difficult to read and follow.
- Use the remembering techniques in Chapter One to help you remember the information in your notes.

# Writing Less without Losing Meaning 3-3

You will not be able to write down everything your teacher says. Teachers speak at about 100–120 words per minute, and high school students write at about 15–20 words per minute.

Read this statement from a lecture. Then answer the two questions.

> The Mississippi River rises in the lake region of northern Minnesota and flows nearly four thousand miles southward through several states until it flows into the Gulf of Mexico through a large delta in southeast Louisiana.

1. How many words are in the statement?

2. How many letters are in the statement?

Read these directions for writing less without losing meaning.

- Write only the words needed to record the ideas presented.
- Use symbols for words (e.g., & for *and*).
- Use standard abbreviations (*FL* for *Florida*) or your own abbreviations (*info* for *information*) for words.

Following these directions, rewrite the statement about the Mississippi River.

Now answer these questions.

3. How many words and symbols are there in your rewritten statement?

4. How many letters are there now?

5. What has this activity taught you about taking notes?

# Forming Abbreviations

A good way to increase your notetaking speed is to write using abbreviations. When using abbreviations for notetaking, it is important to write abbreviations whose meaning you will be able to recognize later. Here are some common words and their standard abbreviations.

| Word | Abbreviation | Word | Abbreviation |
| --- | --- | --- | --- |
| psychology | psy | medicine | med |
| English | Eng | diameter | dia |
| month | mo | year | yr |
| vocabulary | vocab | Illinois | IL |

Write an abbreviation for each of the following words. You can use a standard abbreviation if you know one, or you can create one of your own. Be sure you can recognize the word from the abbreviation you create.

| | |
| --- | --- |
| September | pound |
| tropical | bibliography |
| chemistry | chapter |
| national | street |
| secretary | telephone |
| anatomy | avenue |
| general | kilogram |
| manager | hour |
| auditorium | veterinarian |
| science | page |
| mathematics | Thursday |
| gallon | lieutenant |
| feet | amount |
| agency | President |

Write the standard abbreviation for each of the following:

1. United States of America

2. Internal Revenue Service

3. National Aeronautics and Space Agency

4. Central Intelligence Agency

5. North Atlantic Treaty Organization

6. miles per hour

Create your own abbreviation for each of the following:

7. school principal

8. biology textbook

9. homework

10. longitude and latitude

11. historical factor

12. Johnson's cafeteria

13. How wd u abbre "study skills"?

14. Abbre yr fst and L name.

Another way to write quickly is to use symbols for words or terms. Here are some common words and terms and their symbols.

| | | | | | |
|---|---|---|---|---|---|
| % | percent | & | and | + | plus |
| @ | at | # | number | $ | money |
| = | equals, equal to | ? | question | − | minus |
| × | multiply | ∴ | therefore | ∵ | because |
| ÷ | divided by | ≠ | not equal to | \ | difference |
| > | greater than | < | less than | ‖ | parallel |
| ⊥ | perpendicular | ∠ | angle | ° | degree |
| ′ | minute | ″ | second | ¢ | cent |

Use what you know about abbreviations and symbols to rewrite these sentences.

1. The question before the United States Supreme Court is one of ensuring that justice for one group of people is not greater than justice for another group of people.

2. Five percent of one hundred dollars is less than five percent of one thousand dollars.

3. Sam completed the race in less than 25 minutes, 13 seconds, because the track had few angle turns.

4. The difference between parallel lines and perpendicular lines is that parallel lines go in the same direction, whereas perpendicular lines intersect or form right angles.

Teachers organize their ideas in predictable ways. One of those ways is called **topic–list.** The teacher has a topic and a number of ideas that go with the topic. In the lecture, the topic is presented and then followed by a list of ideas. Number words like **one** or **first** and other words like **next, another, then,** and **finally** are used by teachers to **signal** each idea. The Topic–List pattern can also be used to show enumeration or time order.

Read the following shortened lecture. Draw a single line under the topic. Draw double lines under each idea. Circle the signal words.

The Civil War between the northern and southern states did not begin until 1861. However as early as the period of 1816–1823 there were sources of conflict between the north and south. One of the sources of conflict had to do with the building of a national road from east to west across what was then the United States. The southern states were more interested in developing resources in their states than expanding across the continent. Another problem had to do with tariffs on imported goods. The northern states had factories that were able to manufacture the products they needed. This was not true in the agricultural south. The south had to import goods that were manufactured elsewhere. In many cases they bought manufactured goods from other countries. The tariff on imported goods made these products very expensive. Third, much of the taxes paid by the southern states to the United States government was used by the government to increase industrial growth in the northern states. Would you like to pay taxes that helped someone else and not yourself? I wouldn't. Finally, the Bank of the United States was taking away business from private banks in the south. The southern states needed their banks to build factories. When you consider these sources of conflict, the outbreak of the Civil War is not surprising.

Write the notes you would take, using abbreviations and symbols whenever possible.

Another way teachers organize lectures is called **question–answer.** When this organizational pattern is used, the teacher begins by stating a question. In the lecture, one or more answers to the questions are given. During the lecture additional questions may be asked and answers provided. Words like **who, what, where, when, why, how,** and **in what way(s)** signal each question.

Read the following shortened lecture. Draw a single line under each question. Draw double lines under each answer. Circle the signal words.

Think about an element such as gold being cut into pieces that are smaller and smaller. At a certain point the pieces become too small to be seen even with a microscope. Now just imagine you keep doing this cutting until you end up with the smallest piece of matter that still has the chemical properties of gold. What do you call this piece of matter? It is called an atom. An atom is defined as the smallest part of an element that has the chemical properties of that element. All matter is made of atoms. Who do you think first thought about atoms? It wasn't Einstein. It was long before his time. It was the ancient Greeks who first hypothesized about the existence of atoms. It wasn't until the early 1800s that scientists began to get a good understanding of atoms. Does anyone here know the name of the scientist who developed an atomic theory of matter that helped to explain what atoms were? He was English. His name was John Dalton and his theory motivated other scientists to learn more about atoms.

Write the notes you would take, using abbreviations and symbols whenever possible.

# How Lectures Are Organized: Problem—Solution

Sometimes teachers organize their lectures into a **problem—solution** pattern. Usually the problem is presented first, followed by the solution(s). Sometimes the problem is presented at the end of the lecture. Words like **problem, point of dispute, subject of dispute, puzzle, conundrum, enigma, issue, bafflement, tough nut to crack,** and **complication** signal a problem is being presented. Words like **solution, solve, answer, explanation, explication, interpretation, resolve, elucidate, clear up, unravel, work out,** and **untangle** signal a solution is being proposed.

Read the following shortened lecture. Draw a single line under the problem. Draw double lines under each solution. Circle the signal words.

Major cities throughout the world are crowded with motor vehicles. Cars, trucks, buses and motorcycles are everywhere. There are not enough roads to handle all the motor vehicles. This is a problem in most large cities throughout the world. A number of solutions have been proposed to solve this problem. In New York City a large subway system is used to move people from place to place. In Miami an above-ground monorail system was built. In Los Angeles some roads have been built above existing roads to move more traffic. Many cities have passed laws requiring car pooling during rush hour traffic periods. Some places have raised taxes to finance the building of more roads. This is a difficult problem to solve and many large cities have established commissions to come up with better solutions.

Write the notes you would take, using abbreviations and symbols whenever possible.

Another way teachers organize their lectures is called **cause–effect.** Usually the teacher presents the cause and then discusses its effects. Sometimes the effect is presented first and is followed by a discussion of the causes. Words like **since, thus, therefore, because, consequently, accordingly, so, hence, for that reason, inasmuch, on account of, owing to, due to, whereas,** and **as a result** tell you the teacher is using a cause–effect organizational pattern.

Read the following shortened lecture. Draw a single line under the cause. Draw double lines under each effect. Circle the signal words.

For the United States WWII began on December 7, 1941. Tensions had been developing between the United States and Japan for some time. Japan continued to conquer territories in southeast Asia. The United States stopped selling oil to Japan. After a while this embargo applied to other goods. Because Japan feared the United States would block its advances in Southeast Asia, on December 7, 1941 their military forces attacked the United States naval base at Pearl Harbor.

Write the notes you would take using abbreviations and symbols whenever possible.

# How Lectures Are Organized: Compare

**Compare** is another pattern teachers use when they lecture. The compare pattern is used to show both similarities and differences. Words and phrases like **compare, like, similarly, correspondingly, in parallel, equal to,** and **resemble** signal similarities. Words and phrases like **differently, in contrast, in comparison, on the one hand, on the other hand, opposite,** and **on the contrary** signal differences. When you hear words or phrases that express both similarities and differences, you know the compare pattern is being used.

For example, a teacher could use this pattern to show how travel by airplane and train are both alike and different. Similarities are that you can relax as you travel in both and you do not have to do the driving. One difference is the amount of time it will take to get from one place to another.

Read the following shortened lecture. Place [ ] around the statement that tells what is being compared.

Let's compare high school with college. Many of you are near the end of high school and thinking about going to college. In high school you have the same classes every day while in college classes usually meet only two or three times a week. In high school the same students are in most of your classes whereas in college you will find many different students in your classes. In high school you are frequently reminded of your assignments but in college you are told of your assignments on the first day of class only. In both cases you must complete assignments, attend class, and study to succeed.

*List the similarities here:*                   *List the differences here:*

Write the notes you would take, using abbreviations and symbols whenever possible.

Copyright © 1997 by Allyn and Bacon

**59**

**Contrast** is another lecture pattern used by teachers. The contrast pattern is used to show differences only. Words and phrases like **in contrast, however, but, on the other hand, on the contrary, unlike, the opposite of, difference between, antithesis of, counterpart, disparity,** and **distinction** tell you the contrast pattern is being used.

For example, a teacher could use this pattern to show differences between earth science and life science. Earth science is the study of rocks, oceans, volcanoes, earthquakes, atmosphere, and other features of the earth. In contrast, life science is the study of living things and their parts and actions.

Read the following shortened lecture. Place [ ] around the statement that tells what is being contrasted.

The four seasons of the year are very different. The differences between the seasons are most apparent for summer and winter. In the summer there is a long period of daylight, the land mass heats up, and the water is warmer. In contrast, in winter the period of daylight is short, the land mass cools, and the water becomes frigid. Seasons bring changes that people have to adjust to in their daily lives.

List the differences here:

Write the notes you would take using abbreviations and symbols whenever possible.

You can improve your understanding of your notes by constructing a graphic organizer. Graphic organizers show how the ideas in your notes are related. Examine the following common graphic organizers to see how they are used to relate ideas to each other.

**Topic–List**

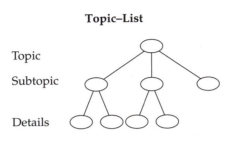

**Question–Answer**

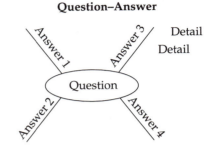

**Problem–Solution**

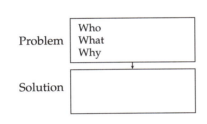

**Cause–Effect**

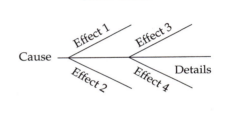

**Compare**

| Similarities | Differences |
|---|---|
|  |  |

**Contrast**

| Differences |
|---|
|  |

In 3-13 you saw how graphic organizers can be used to relate ideas. Use the information presented in 3-2 to complete the following topic–list graphic organizer. "Get Ready" is done for you.

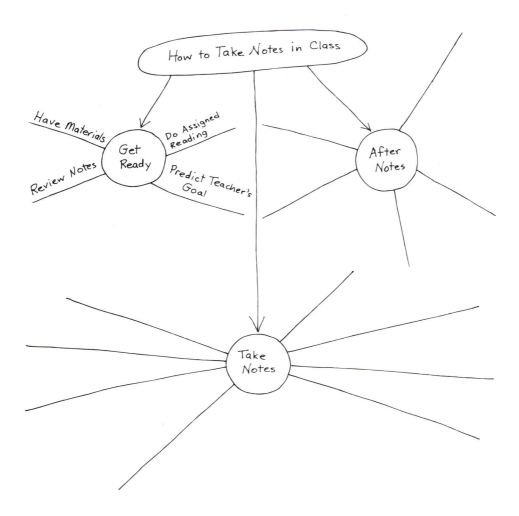

# Two Techniques for Rewriting Notes

Rewrite your notes if they are difficult to read and follow. Some students like to rewrite their notes using words while others like to use graphic organizers. Both work.

Read the original notes from a lecture and the two techniques used to rewrite them.

**Original Notes:**   Confl N & S 1816-1823. 1. bld nat road E 2 W US. 2. tariffs imports. S had to import more th N. Made prod expens. 3. taxes pd by south used in N. 4. US Bank hurt bus S banks.

### Rewritten Word Notes

There were sources of conflict between the N & S from 1816–23 that led to the civil war.

1. N wanted to build national road from east to west across what was then the US. S interested in developing own area—not interested in expanding US.

2. N wanted tariffs on imports so goods made in the US would be cheaper than imports. a. Not a prob for N bec they had fact to make products they needed. b. S mostly farms with few factories. Had to import most manufactured goods. Tarrif added to the cost of goods.

3. Much of taxes paid by S used to develop industries in N.

4. Bank of US (in N) took business away from S banks. S need the money to finance its industrial growth.

### Rewritten Graphic Notes

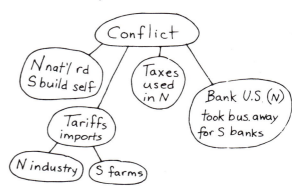

Which technique for rewriting notes would you use?

Why?

For additional practice, rewrite your notes from 3-7 through 3-12. Use one or both of the rewriting techniques shown in 3-15.

See what you have learned about notetaking.

1. Summarize the major ideas for each of the following notetaking stages.
   Get Ready

   Take Notes

   After Notes

2. Write the standard abbreviation for each of the following:

   pound    Illinois    miles per hour    page    gallon    kilogram

3. Write the symbol for each of the following:

   percent    number    money    because    equals    and

4. Write a statement that describes each of these lecture patterns.

   Topic–List
   Question–Answer
   Problem–Solution
   Cause–Effect
   Compare
   Contrast

5. Match each word with the lecture pattern it signals.

   _____ Topic–List          A. solve

   _____ Question–Answer     B. unlike

   _____ Problem–Solution    C. similarly

   _____ Cause–Effect        D. then

   _____ Comparison          E. because

   _____ Contrast            F. what

6. What are the two techniques for rewriting notes?

**3-1** Answers will vary.

**3-2** Answers will vary.

**3-3** 1. 36; 2. 187; 3, 4, 5 Answers will vary.

**3-4** Answers will vary.

**3-5** 1. USA; 2. IRS; 3. NASA; 4. CIA; 5. NATO; 6. mph.
7-14 Answers will vary.

**3-6** Answers will vary. A model is provided for each.
1. ? be4 US Sup Crt 1 of insurng justice 4 1 grp not > 4 ano grp.
2. 5% of $100 < 5% of $1000.
3. Sam compl rce < 25′ 13 ″ ∴ trak few ∠ trns.
4. \ betw | | & ⊥ lnes | | go sme dir & ⊥ intersct or form rght ∠ s.

**3-7** The Civil War between the northern and southern states did not begin until 1861. However as early as the period of 1816–1823 there were <u>sources of conflict between the north and south.</u> (One) of the sources of conflict had to do with the <u>building of a national road</u> from east to west across what was then the United States. The southern states were more interested in developing resources in their states than expanding across the continent. (Another) problem had to do with <u>tariffs on imported goods</u>. The northern states had factories that were able to manufacture the products they needed. This was not true in the agricultural south. The south had to import goods that were manufactured elsewhere. In many cases they bought manufactured goods from other countries. The tariff on imported goods made these products very expensive. (Third,) much of the <u>taxes</u> paid by the southern states to the United States government was <u>used</u> by the government to <u>increase industrial growth in the northern states</u>. Would you like to pay taxes that helped someone else and not yourself? I wouldn't. (Finally,) the <u>Bank of the</u>

United States was taking away business from private banks in the south. The southern states needed their banks to build factories. When you consider these sources of conflict, the outbreak of the Civil War is not surprising.

Notes will vary.

**3-8** Think about an element such as gold being cut into pieces that are smaller and smaller. At a certain point the pieces become too small to be seen even with a microscope. Now just imagine you keep doing this cutting until you end up with the smallest piece of matter that still has the chemical properties of gold. What do you call this piece of matter? It is called an atom. An atom is defined as the smallest part of an element that has the chemical properties of that element. All matter is made of atoms. Who do you think first thought about atoms? It wasn't Einstein. It was long before his time. It was the ancient Greeks who first hypothesized about the existence of atoms. It wasn't until the early 1800s that scientists began to get a good understanding of atoms. Does anyone here know the name of the scientist who developed an atomic theory of matter that helped to explain what atoms were? He was English. His name was John Dalton and his theory motivated other scientists to learn more about atoms.

Notes will vary.

**3-9** Major cities throughout the world are crowded with motor vehicles. Cars, trucks, buses and motorcycles are everywhere. There are <u>not enough roads to handle all the motor vehicles.</u> This is a (problem) in most large cities throughout the world. A number of (solutions) have been proposed to solve this problem. In New York City a large <u>subway system</u> is used to move people from place to place. In Miami an <u>above-ground monorail</u> system was built. In Los Angeles some <u>roads have been built above existing roads</u> to move more traffic. Many cities have passed laws requiring car pooling during rush hour traffic periods. Some places have <u>raised taxes to finance the building of more roads.</u> This is a difficult problem to solve and many large cities have established commissions to come up with better solutions.

Notes will vary.

**3-10** For the United States WWII began on December 7, 1941. Tensions had been developing between the United States and Japan for some time. Japan continued to conquer territories in southeast Asia. The United States stopped selling oil to Japan. After a while this embargo applied to other goods. (Because) <u>Japan feared the United States would block its advances in Southeast Asia</u>, on December 7, 1941 <u>their military forces attacked the United States naval base at Pearl Harbor.</u>

Notes will vary.

**3-11** Let's compare [high school with college]. Many of you are near the end of high school and thinking about going to college. In high school you have the same classes every day while in college classes usually meet only two or three times a week. In high school the same students are in most of your classes whereas in college you will find many different students in your classes. In high school you are frequently reminded of your assignments but in college you are told of your assignments on the first day of class only. In both cases you must complete assignments, attend class, and study to succeed.

| *Similarities* | *Differences* |
|---|---|
| complete assignments | Classes don't meet every day. |
| attend class | Different students in each class. |
| study | No frequent reminders of assignments. |

Notes will vary.

**3-12** The four seasons of the year are very different. The differences between the seasons are most apparent for [summer and winter]. In the summer there is a long period of daylight, the land mass heats up, and the water is warmer. In contrast, in winter the period of daylight is short, the land mass cools, and the water becomes frigid. Seasons bring changes that people have to adjust to in their daily lives.

*Differences*
period of daylight
temperature of land mass
temperature of water

Notes will vary.

**3-14** No writing required.

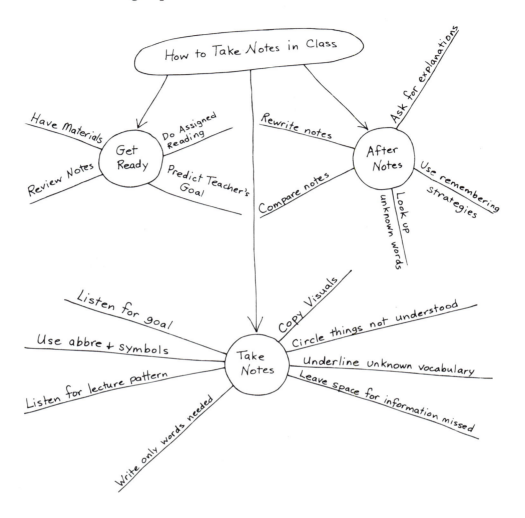

**3-15** Answers will vary.

**3-16** Answers will vary.

**3-17** 1. **Get Ready**
- Have notetaking materials ready.
- Review notes from previous day.
- Do assigned reading for that day's class.
- Predict the teacher's goal for that day's class.

**Take Notes**
- Listen for the teacher's statement of the goal.
- Use abbreviations and symbols.
- Listen for the teacher's lecture pattern.
- Write only the words needed to record the ideas presented.
- Copy information presented visually.
- Circle anything you wrote but did not understand.
- Underline unknown words and terms.
- Leave blanks for information missed.

**After Notes**

- Ask your teacher or other students to explain things in your notes you do not understand. Make the changes in your notes.
- Use the glossary or a dictionary to define unknown words and terms. Write the definitions in the margin.
- Compare your notes with those of other students to fill-in any blanks. Go to the textbook or your teacher if you still need help.
- Rewrite your notes if they are difficult to read and follow.
- Use the remembering techniques in Chapter One to help you remember the information in your notes.

2. pound lb; Illinois IL; miles per hour mph; page p; gallon gal; kilogram kg.
3. percent %; number #; money $; because ∴;   equals =; and &.
4. *Topic–List:* A topic is presented and followed by a list of ideas.
   *Question–Answer:* A question is presented and followed by one or more answers.
   *Problem–Solution:* A problem is presented and followed by a solution or solutions.
   *Cause–Effect:* A cause is presented and followed by a discussion of its effects.
   *Compare:* Similarities and differences are shown for two things.
   *Contrast:* Only differences are shown for two things.
5. Topic–List D; Question–Answer F; Problem–Solution A; Cause–Effect E; Compare C; Contrast B.
6. Rewritten word notes. Rewritten graphic notes.

# Using the Library and the Internet to Locate Information

## CHAPTER OBJECTIVES

1. Teach students to use the library and the Internet to locate information.
2. Teach students to evaluate the information they locate.

## TITLES OF REPRODUCIBLE ACTIVITIES

## USING THE REPRODUCIBLE ACTIVITIES

After you have distributed a reproducible activity, here are suggestions for its use. Feel free to add further information, illustrations or examples. Wherever possible, relate the activity to actual subject area assignments.

### 4-1 A Strategy for Using the Library and the Internet

Invite the librarian to your class. Ask the librarian to discuss with students how today's library contains information in both print and electronic form. Have the librarian guide students through the flowchart and define any terms students do not know. Then have students answer the questions on their own.

### 4-2 Formats of Information

Review the four formats and have students complete the activity.

### 4-3 Types of Materials Found in a Library

Describe each of the types of materials found in a library. Provide examples of each type where possible. Then have students complete the matching activity.

### 4-4 Your Library Catalog—Card and Online

Invite the librarian to your class. Ask the librarian to explain the difference between a card catalog and an online catalog. Then have students ask the librarian the questions necessary to complete the activity. As an alternative send the students to the library to consult with the librarian.

### 4-5 Learning about the Card Catalog

Even if your school library does not have a card catalog, use this activity. Your students may use other local libraries that still have card catalogs and will need to know about the three types of cards found in the card catalog. .Explain why three cards are necessary. Then have students answer the questions.

### 4-6 Learning about the Online Catalog

Review with the students the record from the online catalog. Define fields as categories of information found on the left side of the record. On the right side of the record students will find information for each field. Review with students the various fields in the record and the types of information in each. Have students answer the questions.

### 4-7 Using Your Online Catalog

Note: Skip this activity if your library does not have an online catalog.

Invite the librarian to your class. Ask the librarian to explain what you can find using the online catalog in the school library. Then have students ask the librarian the questions necessary to complete the activity. As an alternative, send the students to the library to consult with the librarian.

### 4-8 Learning about the Dewey Decimal System

Review the Dewey Decimal System with the students and have them complete the activity.

### 4-9 Learning about the Library of Congress System

Review the Library of Congress system with the students and have them complete the activity.

### 4-10 Locating Books by Call Number

Use the example to show students how call numbers in the Dewey Decimal System are arranged in numerical order. Then have students complete the Dewey Decimal ordering activity. Use the next example to show students how Library of Congress call numbers are arranged in alphanumerical order. Have students complete the ordering activity.

### 4-11 Learning about Print Indexes

Have students read about print indexes and answer the questions.

### 4-12 Using Print Indexes

Tell students they will find citations in indexes. Use the example to explain what is typically found in a citation. Point out to students that their library may not have the publication described in a citation. Then have students complete the labeling activity.

### 4-13 Locating Print Indexes

Have students go to the library to locate the information needed to complete the activity. Remind them to consult with the librarian as necessary.

### 4-14 Using CD ROM Databases

Emphasize to students that a CD ROM index contains all the information found in a print index. Point out that often the CD ROM index contains an abstract, and sometimes it has the full text of articles cited. Have students examine the sample CD ROM record and then answer the questions.

### 4-15 Locating CD ROM Databases

Note: Skip this activity if your library does not have CD ROM databases.

Have students go to the library to locate CD ROM databases needed to answer the questions. Point out to students that they may find databases other than the ones listed. Remind them to consult with the librarian as necessary.

### 4-16 Using Boolean Search Connectors

Boolean connectors show how different sets of information are related. Use the examples and their diagrams to explain how the words **and, or, not** are used to narrow and/or broaden searches for information on a topic. Use the example of a multiple connector to show how a Boolean connector can be used more than once in the same search. Then have students draw diagrams to demonstrate their understanding.

### 4-17 Using Keywords in Computer Searches

Emphasize the importance of selecting appropriate keywords. Have students select four keywords to use in a search for information about the topic. Then use the example for the keyword **teenager** to explain how students must use other forms of the keyword as well as synonyms and related terms.

### 4-18 Learning about the Internet

Review the introductory text on "What Is the Internet?" with your students. Clarify words and concepts as necessary. Direct the students to answer questions 1–3. Next, review the text "What Can You Do on the Internet?" Direct the students to answer questions 4–9.

### 4-19  Using the World Wide Web

Go over the introductory text with the students. Review the information on the NASA home page. Point out that home pages vary considerably. Have students answer the questions about the NASA home page. Encourage students to bring in examples of other home pages to share with the class.

### 4-20  Learning about Your Local FreeNet

Use this activity only if your community has a local FreeNet. Check with your public library if you are uncertain.

Begin by discussing the introductory text with your students. Have the students look at the choices on the sample FreeNet menu. Direct the students to complete the activity. You can extend this activity by bringing in a menu from your own local FreeNet.

### 4-21  Question the Source

Lead students in a discussion about the sources from which they can obtain information. Have students write sources of information for the four locations. Then have students rate the believability of each source using the scale provided.

### 4-22  Question the Source—An Internet Exercise

Note: Use this activity only if your school provides access to the World Wide Web (WWW).

Explain to students that because there is little control over the accuracy of the information placed on the Internet, they need to learn how to evaluate the information provided. Explain the URL and its important parts. Have students locate information on the WWW and record the URL. Take students through the five procedures for evaluating the believability of a source and information provided by the source. Then have students use the scale provided to rate the believability of the information they found.

### 4-23  Chapter Four Mastery Assessment

Have students complete this assessment at any point you believe they have learned how to use the library. Review the results of the assessment with the students. Provide additional instruction as necessary.

# A Strategy for Using the Library and the Internet

The first place to look for information is the library. Librarians are there to help you. Most libraries also provide computer systems to help you locate information. Many libraries provide access to the Internet, a worldwide computer network that allows you to find information on computers all over the world. Examine the flowchart showing the paths you can follow to locate information.

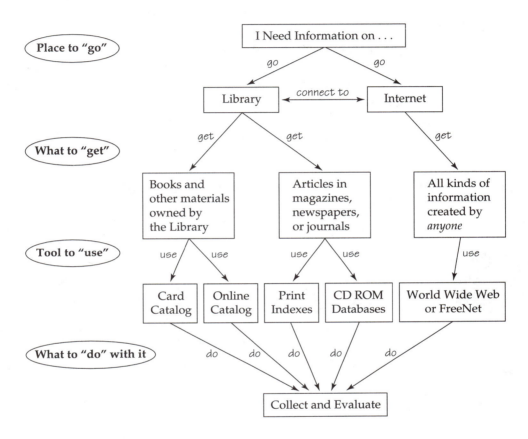

Use the flowchart to answer the questions.

1. Where are two places to go to locate information?

2. What sources of information will you find in the library?

3. On the Internet?

4. What tools can you use to locate information in the library?

5. On the Internet?

6. What should you do with information once you locate it?

Copyright © 1997 by Allyn and Bacon

**77**

Information in a library is packaged in many different ways. The way information is packaged is called a format. Four major formats are:

Print          Print format uses paper. Examples are books, magazines, newspapers, and pamphlets.

Electronic     Electronic formats use a computer to deliver information. Electronic formats include CD ROM and the Internet.

Audio/Visual   A/V formats require you to watch or listen. Examples include slides, films, audiocassettes, and videocassettes.

Microform      Microform formats reduce an image and put it on plastic to be read in a machine. Microfilm, microfiche, and microcartridge are examples of microforms.

Write the name of the format that goes with each illustration.

1.

2.

3.

4.

5.

6.

Many different types of materials are found in libraries. On the line in front of each type of material, write the letter corresponding to its description.

**Material**

1. _____ government documents

2. _____ books

3. _____ magazines

4. _____ audiocassettes

5. _____ CD ROM

6. _____ microfiche

7. _____ journals

8. _____ reference books

9. _____ microfilm

10. _____ newspapers

11. _____ multimedia

12. _____ videocassettes

**Description**

A. Flat plastic cards, usually 4' × 6', with reduced images, read or copied on reader/printers.

B. A collection of articles written by experts in a specific field and published at regular intervals throughout the year, usually monthly or quarterly.

C. Materials to help you do research such as encyclopedias, almanacs, directories, and indexes. Usually these materials cannot be taken from the library.

D. Cartridge containing magnetic tape with a filmed or televised image, usually including sound, and viewed using a television monitor and VCR.

E. Small reels of plastic film that contain a reduced image, read or copied on reader/printers.

F. Small cartridge containing magnetic tape with recorded speech or sounds, and listened to using a tape recorder.

G. A daily publication containing news and opinions about current events, feature stories, and advertising.

H. Compact Disc Read Only Memory. A computer-based method of storing information as a database, requiring a computer and CD player for use.

I. Materials published by local, state, federal, and international governments.

J. Extensive coverage of a subject printed on paper that is bound together in a single volume.

K. CD ROM database that uses full text, video, sound, animation, color, and other features to provide information. Many reference books and encyclopedias are now available in this format.

L. A weekly or monthly publication, usually with glossy pictures and advertisements, containing articles written by journalists on topics of general interest.

All libraries have a catalog listing materials found in the library. The catalog describes each item and tells where it is located. Some libraries have a **card catalog** where the information is typed on 3″ × 5″ cards and arranged alphabetically in file drawers. The file drawers are arranged in cabinets that look like this:

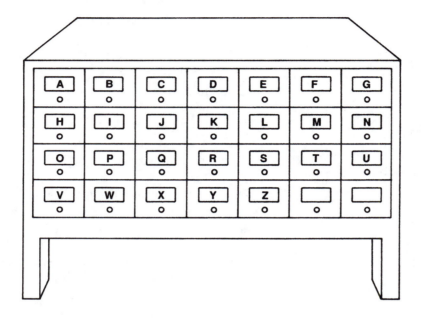

Use the information provided by the librarian to answer the questions.

1. Does your library have a card catalog?     Yes   No

2. If yes, circle the items found by using your library's card catalog.

| | | |
|---|---|---|
| books | magazines | films |
| maps | videocassettes | journals |
| audiocassettes | newspapers | government documents |

Instead of a card catalog, some libraries have an **online** catalog where the information is entered into a computer. Most libraries name their online catalogs.

3. Does your library have an online catalog?     Yes     No

4. If yes, does your online catalog have a name?     Yes     No

   Write its name here:

A card catalog lists all the items found in the library. Information about each item is typed on a card and filed alphabetically in drawers. Each item has three cards to allow you to look for it in different ways. You can look for an item by subject, title, or author.

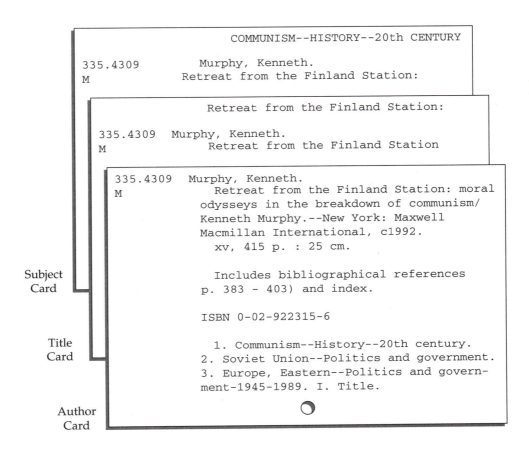

1. Under what subjects could you find this book?

2. What is its title?

3. Who wrote it?

4. In what year was it published?

5. Who is the publisher?

6. How many pages are there?

7. Are there any bibliographical references?

8. Does the book have an index?

Here is an example of a computer record in an online catalog. Whereas there are three types of cards for each item in a card catalog, there is only one computer record for each item in an online catalog. The information on a computer record is arranged in **fields.**

*Field*                          *Information in each Field*

| | |
|---|---|
| Author: | Cutlip, Glen W. |
| Title: | Learning and Information: skills for the secondary classroom and library media program/ Glen W. Cutlip; edited by Paula Kay Montgomery. |
| Imprint: | Englewood, Colo. : Libraries Unlimited, 1988 |
| Call Number: | 025.5 |
| Physical features: | xvii, 134 p. : ill.; 28 cm. |
| Series: | Teaching library media research and information skills series |
| Notes: | Includes bibliography (p. 121–130) and index. |
| Other authors: | Montgomery, Paula Kay |
| Subjects: | Library orientation of high school students |
| | High school libraries |
| | Media programs (Education) |
| ISBN: | 0872875806 |
| OCLC no. | 18987516 |

1. Under what subjects could you find this book?

2. What is its title?

3. Who wrote it?

4. In what year was it published?

5. Who is the publisher?

6. How many pages are there?

7. Are there any bibliographical references?

8. Does the book have an index?

Check what you can find using your online catalog.

_____  What years of a newspaper the library has.

_____  If a book is checked out.

_____  The latest issue of a magazine that the library received.

_____  If a new book has been ordered.

_____  Materials found in other libraries.

_____  References to articles *in* magazines.

_____  References to articles *in* newspapers.

_____  The whole article from a magazine or newspaper or reference book.

Does your online catalog have a connection to:

_____  A FreeNet?

_____  The Internet?

If your school library has a card catalog, describe how it is different from an online catalog.

Most school libraries are organized using the Dewey Decimal System. Books on similar subjects are grouped together under ten primary classes. The primary classes are represented by numbers. Here are the ten primary classes and the numbers that go with each.

| | | | |
|---|---|---|---|
| 000–099 | Generalities | 500–599 | Pure Science |
| 100–199 | Philosophy and Related | 600–699 | Technology (Applied Sciences) |
| 200–299 | Religion | 700–799 | The Arts |
| 300–399 | The Social Sciences | 800–899 | Literature and Rhetoric |
| 400–499 | Language | 900–999 | General Geography and History, etc. |

Under which numbers would you find books on the following topics:

1. the artist Picasso _____

2. chemistry _____

3. Christianity _____

4. French terms _____

5. the *Encyclopedia Britannica* _____

6. fall of the Roman Empire _____

7. the philosopher Plato _____

8. the playwright Shakespeare _____

9. social welfare _____

10. using robots _____

# Learning about the Library of Congress System

The Library of Congress, located in Washington, D.C., is the largest library in the United States. The system developed to organize this library is called the Library of Congress (LC) system. The LC system is used in many other libraries. Books on similar subjects are grouped together under twenty primary classes. The primary classes are represented by letters of the alphabet. Here are the twenty primary classes of the LC system and the letter(s) that goes with each.

| | | | |
|---|---|---|---|
| General Works | A | Music | M |
| Philosophy, Psychology, Religion | B | Fine Arts | N |
| Archaeology, Genealogy, Biography | C | Language and Literature | P |
| History: General and Old World | D | Sciences | Q |
| History: Americas | E–F | Medicine | R |
| Geography, Anthropology, Recreation | G | Agriculture | S |
| Social Sciences | H | Technology | T |
| Political Sciences | J | Military Science | U |
| Law | K | Naval Science | V |
| Education | L | Bibliography, Library Science | Z |

Indicate under what letter you would find books on the following topics:

1. _____ Civil War

2. _____ Spanish Novels

3. _____ Buddhism

4. _____ Public School Curriculum

5. _____ Sports

6. _____ Rock and Roll

7. _____ Michelangelo

8. _____ Government

When you locate an entry for a book in a card or online catalog, the book will be identified by a **call number.** A call number is a series of numbers or numbers and letters typed on a label on a book. They tell the subject of the book and the place where the book belongs on the shelf.

In 4-8 you learned how numbers in the **Dewey Decimal System** tell you about the subject of a book. In this activity you will learn how to use a call number to locate a book on the shelf. By knowing how call numbers are arranged in numerical order, you will be able to quickly locate a book on the shelf.

Call numbers in the Dewey Decimal System use numbers and decimals. Look at these Dewey Decimal call numbers. They have been placed in correct numerical order.

( 1 ) 338.7　　( 2 ) 338.7016　　( 3 ) 338.74
( 4 ) 338.8　　( 5 ) 338.88　　( 6 ) 338.973

**1.** Now use the numbers 1–6 to show the correct order of these call numbers.

(　) 306.8　　　　(　) 306.36　　　(　) 306.4812
(　) 306.09759　　(　) 306.08　　　(　) 306.1

In 4-9 you learned how letters in the **Library of Congress System** tell you about the subject of a book. Here you will learn how to use these letters along with numbers and decimals to locate a book. The combination of letters and numbers is called **alphanumeric.** Look at these Library of Congress call numbers. They have been placed in correct alphanumerical order.

| JK | JK | JK | JK | JK |
|----|----|----|----|----|
| 560 | 560 | 560 | 562 | 570 |
| .G78 | .R68 | .R7 | .R5 | .G46 |

**2.** Now use the numbers 1–5 to show the correct order of these call numbers.

| HD | HD | HD | HD | HD |
|----|----|----|----|----|
| 8066 | 8066 | 806 | 8066. | 806.6 |
| .L38 | .L3 | .L298 | .L3224 | .L34 |
| (　) | (　) | (　) | (　) | (　) |

Indexes are used to locate articles in periodicals and newspapers. Periodicals are published regularly—weekly, monthly, or at other regular intervals throughout the year. Magazines and journals are types of periodicals. Newspapers are also published at regular intervals, daily or weekly. Indexes help you locate articles on any topic in thousands of periodicals and newspapers. In addition to identifying articles about a topic, some indexes also include an **abstract,** or short summary, of an article.

Libraries own many indexes in **print** format. Print indexes look like books and are used to look up a topic. Each volume in an index covers a certain period of time. Usually an index covers a specific year. Some indexes date back as far back as 1900.

1. What is the purpose of an index?

2. What is an abstract?

3. Are magazines periodicals?

4. How often are periodicals published?

5. How often are newspapers published?

Many libraries also own indexes in electronic format, usually on **CD ROM.** A computer and CD player are required to use an index on CD ROM. A CD ROM index is also called a **database.** The database often includes many years on a single disc. In addition to including an abstract, many of these databases also include the full text of an article. Because CD ROM is a relatively new technology, most CD ROM databases go back only as far as the 1980s.

6. What is another name for a CD ROM index?

7. Can you have articles from different years on a single disc?

8. Can you use a CD ROM database without a computer?

9. If you want to find magazine articles for the year 1945, would you use a print index or a CD ROM database?

10. Why do CD ROM databases go back only as far as the 1980s?

# Using Print Indexes

**Print indexes** provides citations to articles about a topic. A **citation** is the information that completely identifies a publication. For a magazine or newspaper article, the citation usually includes the author, title of the article, title of the publication, volume, issue, date of publication, and the page numbers. Often the titles of publications are abbreviated. The abbreviated titles are listed in the front of the index volume with their full titles.

Follow these steps when using a print index to locate information about a topic.

1. Identify citations related to the topic.
2. Check to see if the publication included in a citation is available in the library.

Here is an example of a citation with its parts labeled.

Title ─────► Information literacy for high school students

Author ─────► P. Brownuzzi. **Secondary School News** 3(8): 9–18 Ag 8 '95

Magazine

Volume
Issue
Pages
Month
Day
Year

Here is another example. Label each part.

_____ ─────► Electronic libraries in schools

_____ ─────► W.E Braunsfelsia. **School INTERNET Review** 1(4): 12–28 D '95

There are many print indexes. Some are general indexes covering all topics in popular magazines. Others are indexes to newspapers. You will also find specialized indexes for specific subjects. Here are some frequently used print indexes:

General indexes
- Readers Guide to Periodical Literature
- General Science Index
- Humanities Index
- Social Sciences Index

Newspaper indexes
- NewsBank
- New York Times Index
- Wall Street Journal Index
- Index to the Christian Science Monitor

Specialized indexes
- Art Index
- Music Index
- Applied Science and Technology Index
- Education Index

Go to the library to learn about the print indexes it owns. Then complete the following:

1. The title of a general index in my library is

2. The dates owned for this general index are

3. The title of a newspaper index in my library is

4. The dates owned for this newspaper index are

5. The title of a specialized index in my library is

6. The dates owned for this specialized index are

Like print indexes, **CD ROM databases** provide citations to articles about a topic. All the information from a print index is included in a CD ROM database. In addition, the CD ROM database includes the abstract of an article and sometimes the whole article. Citations are entered onto a CD ROM to create a **record.** There is one record per article. The information on the computer record is arranged in fields. You can find information in the CD ROM database by searching under any field: author, title (source or headline), subject (index terms), date, and others.

## SAMPLE CD ROM RECORD

(CD Newsworld International (January 1, 1996 - March 31, 1996)

Source:         The Aurora Times

Headline:       Standing Up For Music: Rapsters and Fans Defend Their Music

Date:           November 12, 1995          Section:   Arts, Entertainment

Page:           D2                          Edition:   Final

Graphic:        Photo                       Length:    750 words

Index Terms:    rap music

                censorship

Answer these questions using the sample record.

1. What is the title of this article?

2. Where was the article published?

3. When was the article published?

4. What is the name of the database used to locate this record?

5. What was the article about?

6. What type of visual was included in the article?

7. Was the article in the main section of the newspaper?

8. Can you tell who wrote the article?

There are many CD ROM databases. Some are general databases covering all topics found in popular magazines. Others are databases for newspapers. You will also find specialized databases for specific subjects. Here are some frequently used CD ROM databases:

| | |
|---|---|
| General databases | Wilson's Readers Guide Abstracts |
| | IAC Magazine Index on Infotrac |
| | UMI Periodical Abstracts Ondisc |
| | SIRS Researcher CD ROM (Social Issues Research Services) |
| | |
| Newspaper databases | NewsBank Comprehensive CD ROM |
| | Ethnic Newswatch |
| | UMI Newspaper Abstracts Ondisc |
| | (University Microfilms International) |
| | |
| Specialized databases | IAC Health Reference Center on Infotrac |
| | (Information Access Company) |
| | ERIC (Education Resources Information Clearinghouse) |
| | Computer Library |

Go to the library to learn about the CD ROM databases it owns. Then complete the following:

1. The title of a general database on CD ROM in my library is


2. The dates this CD ROM covers are


3. The title of a newspaper database on CD ROM in my library is


4. The dates this CD ROM covers are


5. The title of a specialized database on CD ROM in my library is


6. The dates this CD ROM covers are

# Using Boolean Search Connectors

Computer databases use **Boolean connectors** to search for information. Boolean Connectors are **and, or,** and **not.** They are used and diagrammed as follows:

| Connector | Use | Diagram | Example |
|---|---|---|---|
| **and** | Focus or narrow a search | | rap **and** violence |
| **or** | Expand or broaden a search | | rap **or** hip-hop |
| **not** | Exclude specific terms | | rap **not** hip-hop |

Sometimes a connector may be used more than once in the same search as shown here.

| Connectors | Use | Diagram | Example |
|---|---|---|---|
| **and, and** | Focus or narrow search | | rap **and** concerts **and** violence |

Draw the diagram that illustrates each connector:

1. computers **or** technology

2. computers **and** games

3. computers **and** education **and** games

4. computers **not** games

To do a computer search on a topic, begin by selecting an important word about the topic. This word is a keyword. You can use more than one keyword to focus your search. However, remember to use a Boolean connector when using more than one keyword. When you enter the keyword(s) into the database, the computer will list all records that contain the keyword(s). You can then choose to look at the records that are most related to your topic. These records can be used to identify additional keywords to use in your search. The subject field of the record is an excellent source of additional keywords.

Examine the sample record that was generated by entering the keywords **information** and **literacy** in a search for information about information literacy. Use the sample record to identify four additional keywords to find information about the topic.

1. _____    2. _____    3. _____    4. _____

Sample Computer Record

| | |
|---|---|
| Author | Brownuzzi, Patricia |
| Title: | Information literacy for high school students |
| Found in: | Secondary School News 3(8): 9–18 Ag 8 '95 |
| Abstract: | If students wish to succeed in society today, they must acquire three basic literacy skills: literacy; computer literacy; and information literacy. A solid foundation of reading skills is just the beginning. Students must also acquire basic skills in using a personal computer in a networked environment. We are evolving from a print to a digital information society, and students must learn how to identify, evaluate, select, and use the information that they find in both print and electronic formats. |
| Subjects: | High school students — Library orientation |
| | High school libraries |
| | Computer literacy |
| | Libraries and society |

Computers do exactly what you tell them to do. If you ask the computer to search for the keyword **teenager** it will find all the records with the keyword **teenager.** It will NOT find other forms of the keyword **teenager,** such as **teen.** It will NOT find synonyms for **teenager,** such as **adolescent.** If you want other forms of a keyword and/or synonyms for a keyword, you must use Boolean connectors. For example:

teenagers    **or**    teenager    **or**    teens    **or**    adolescents

Write another form of the keyword **school** and as many synonyms and related terms as you can for this keyword. Use a dictionary or thesaurus as needed.

| *Keyword* | *Other Forms* | *Synonyms and Related Terms* |
|---|---|---|
| school | | |

The **Internet** is a worldwide network of large computers that are connected to each other. These large computers are located at colleges and universities, research institutions, government agencies, and private corporations. The Internet allows you to use your personal computer to connect to and use information on these large computers. The Internet has been called the **information superhighway** because it is like a road (network) that can get you to places (computers).

1. What is the Internet?

2. How is the Internet like a highway?

3. At what locations can you find the large computers that are on the Internet?

## WHAT CAN YOU DO ON THE INTERNET?

The Internet offers several services such as **e-mail, gopher,** and the **World Wide Web (WWW).** You can send an e-mail (electronic mail) message to anyone in the world who has a connection to the Internet. The message will appear in their "mailbox" on their computer. You can also use e-mail to join a discussion group to chat with others about similar interests. Gopher uses menus to search the Internet. You find information by making selections from the menus. The WWW allows you to jump from one Internet location to another by clicking on **linked** words, phrases, or images which are connected to other pages of information. You need a **web browser** and an account on the Internet to use the WWW. Some web browsers present graphic images in addition to text. Others present text only.

4. Which Internet service uses menus to search for information?

5. What does e-mail stand for?

6. Why would you join an Internet discussion group?

7. What does WWW stand for?

8. What are linked words?

9. What is needed to use the WWW?

# Using the World Wide Web

The **World Wide Web (WWW)** is the most popular way to explore the Internet. Information on the WWW is organized on **web pages.** The first or top page in a set of web pages is called the **home page.** The WWW is a **hypertext** system. This means you can click on a highlighted (hot) word, phrase, or image on a web page to jump to another place where you will find information related to that word, phrase, or image. Here is an example of a web page.

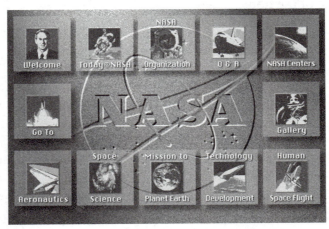

National Aeronautics and Space Administration

 **The NASA Homepage**

- Welcome - This is a good place to begin your journey. Start by reading a letter from NASA Administrator, Dan Goldin, or NASA's Strategic Plan. Check out the User Tips page to find the helper applications you will need to get the most out of what we have to offer. If you're looking for something specific, there's a search engine for the top-level NASA pages.
- Today@NASA - If you've read about NASA recently or seen something on TV, this is place to go for links to more details about breaking news. You can find the most recent Hubble Space Telescope Images, links to the Shuttle Web and the latest news releases. [This site is extremely busy, please be patient.]
- NASA Organization - A list of the offices at NASA Headquarters with links to their Web sites. Below this list, you'll find an extensive subject index of NASA Web sites.
- Questions and Answers - Have you ever wondered where you can order NASA photographs? Or how to become an astronaut? Or how to see a launch? This is the place to go to find the most commonly sought information about the U.S. space program.
- NASA Centers - Most of NASA's work is done at the agency's field centers. Here you'll find links to their Home Pages.
- Go To - Links back to the NASA Organization, the NASA Centers, other nations' space agencies and other U.S. federal agencies.
- Gallery - Video, audio clips and still images are here for the downloading.
- Aeronautics - An overview of NASA's aeronautics research and links to related Webs.
- Space Science - What lies beyond our home world? Here's information on NASA's planetary exploration, astronomy and research into the origins of life.
- Mission to Planet Earth - Dedicated to understanding the many ways the Earth is constantly changing and how human beings influence those changes.
- Technology Development - NASA is dedicated to improving U.S. technological capability through innovative developments. Here's where you'll find information on that effort, including reducing the cost of access to space and technology transfer.
- Human Space Flight - This Web provides links to the Office of Space Flight, including the Space Shuttle and Space Station Home Pages, and the Office of Life and Microgravity Sciences, which conducts research aboard the Shuttle and is planning experiments for the Space Station.

You can send us comments or questions about our Web site to *comments@www.hq.nasa.gov*
*Author: Brian Dunbar    Curator: Jim Gass    WebSite Design: Stephen E. Chambers*

Refer to the sample web page to answer the following questions:

1. Some web pages have navigation buttons that you can click on to jump to another page of information. "Mission to Planet Earth" is one of the navigation buttons on the sample page. Write the name of another navigation button.

2. What is the name of the home page?

3. The home page usually provides some information about the organization or individual who created the web page(s). What organization is responsible for the information on this home page?

4. On the computer screen, hot words or phrases are highlighted in different colors from the rest of the text. These words or phrases are underlined when printed. Write at least three hot words or phrases found on the NASA home page.

5. The bottom of a web page often provides information about the individual who designed, created, or wrote the page. Who are the people responsible for the NASA home page? Write their names and titles.

6. Web pages often include a link to the e-mail address of the creator or author. This link allows visitors traveling on the information superhighway who stop by for a visit to send comments or otherwise communicate with the author. What is the e-mail address provided on the NASA home page?

A FreeNet is a computer information system for your town or city. There are FreeNets through-out the United States and all over the world. FreeNets provide a free connection to the Internet. This connection may allow you to send and receive e-mail and to use menus to search for infor-mation on the WWW. In most cases, however, you will not be able to view the graphics accom-panying the information on a web page. Following is an example of a FreeNet menu.

```
SEFLIN FREE-NET — DADE COUNTY EDITION (menu = main)
   1. About SEFLIN Free-Net (Administration)        (admin)
   2. Around the Network (INDEX)                     (index)
   3. Arts & Entertainment (District)                (arts)
   4. Business & Industrial Park                     (business)
   5. Comm Central (Mailbox, Teleport, Newsstand)    (cc)
   6. Education Center                               (school)
   7. Government & Communities Information Complex   (govern)
   8. Home, Garden, & Daily Living                   (home)
   9. Legal, Financial & Tax Building                (legal)
  10. Library & Literary Complex                     (library)
  11. Medical & Health Center                        (health)
  12. Religion & Philosophy Center                   (religion)
  13. Science & Technology Center                    (science)
  14. Social Services Complex                        (social)
  15. Special Interest Groups                        (special)
  16. Sports Arena & Recreation Center               (sports)
  17. Youth Center                                   (teen)
```

Write the number from the FreeNet menu that you would select to do each of the following:

1. _____ Find restaurant reviews for your town.

2. _____ Join an electronic discussion group about sports.

3. _____ Find information about hinduism.

4. _____ Have questions answered from your local tax office.

5. _____ Find out about career opportunities.

6. _____ Find out about the welfare system.

7. _____ Connect to the U.S. Department of Agriculture home page.

8. _____ Have your own e-mail account.

9. _____ Connect to library online catalogs all over the world.

10. _____ Find out what happened at the board of commissioners meeting.

11. _____ Share opinions with other teenagers in your town about music.

# Question the Source

Think about where you get information when you are in each of the following places. List at least five sources of information for each place.

**At Home**

1. _____ (  )

2. _____ (  )

3. _____ (  )

4. _____ (  )

5. _____ (  )

**In the Car**

1. _____ (  )

2. _____ (  )

3. _____ (  )

4. _____ (  )

5. _____ (  )

**At School**

1. _____ (  )

2. _____ (  )

3. _____ (  )

4. _____ (  )

5. _____ (  )

**At the Library**

1. _____ (  )

2. _____ (  )

3. _____ (  )

4. _____ (  )

5. _____ (  )

Some sources of information are more **believable** than others. Rate the believability of each source according to the following scale. Write your rating inside the (  ).

**1** Not believable
**2** Possibly believable
**3** Believable

# Question the Source—An Internet Exercise

Anyone can make information available on the Internet. That's why you need to know how to evaluate the believability of the source of any information you find on the WWW. Use this activity after you have found information using the WWW.

1. The URL ("uniform resource locator") is the "address" of a Web site. Write down the URL for the site where you located the information. It usually starts with:

   http:// _____

2. Look at your URL to see if it has any of the following parts. These parts tell something about the source of the information. Here are some parts you might find. Does your URL have one of these parts? If YES, circle it.

   .com                    .gov                    .edu                    .org

   com = commercial    gov = government    edu = education    org = organization

3. Look at the top of the home page. Is there anything that identifies the source of the information? A company or person or organization? If YES, write the name of the person or organization here.

4. Look at the bottom of the page. Is there a name for the source who wrote or provided the information? Is there any other information about the company, person, or organization? If YES, write it here.

5. Look at the bottom of the page. It should say "this page maintained by . . ." and should give the name and address of this person. If YES, write the name and address here.

6. Some sources of information are more **believable** than others. Rate the believability of your source of the information by circling one of the following:

   1   Not believable
   2   Possibly believable
   3   Believable

7. Why did you assign this rating?

Copyright © 1997 by Allyn and Bacon

**99**

# Chapter Four Mastery Assessment

See what you have learned about using the library and the Internet to locate information:

1. What should you do with information once you locate it?

2. What are the four major **formats of information?**

3. What is the difference between a **card catalog** and an **online catalog?**

4. What are the three different types of cards found in a **card catalog?**

5. In what way is the information on a **computer record** arranged?

6. How many primary classes does the **Dewey Decimal System** include?

7. How many primary classes does the **Library of Congress System** include?

8. What two things are done by **call numbers?**

9. What is a **CD ROM database?**

10. What is a **citation?**

11. What two steps should you follow when using an **index?**

12. Which **Boolean connector** would you use to expand a computer database search?   to exclude specific terms?      to narrow a search?

13. What is a **keyword?**

14. What is the **Internet?**

15. What is a **FreeNet?**

16. One of four major parts may appear in a **URL.** What are these four major parts?

**4-1** 1. Library; Internet.
    2. Books; articles in magazines, newspapers, or journals.
    3. All kinds of information created by anyone.
    4. Card catalog; online catalog; print indexes; CD ROM databases.
    5. World Wide Web or FreeNet.
    6. Collect and evaluate the information.

**4-2** 1. Microfilm.  2. Compact Disc.  3. Book.
    4. Videocassette.  5. Magazine.  6. Microfiche.

**4-3** 1. I; 2. J; 3. L; 4. F; 5. H; 6. A; 7. B; 8. C; 9. E; 10. G; 11. K; 12. D.

**4-4** Answers will vary.

**4-5** 1. Communism-history-twentieth century; 2. "Retreat from the Finland Station." 3. Kenneth Murphy. 4. 1992. 5. Maxwell Macmillan International. 6. 415. 7. Yes. 8. Yes.

**4-6** 1. Library orientation of high school students; High school libraries; Media programs (Education).
    2. "Learning and Information: Skills for the Secondary Classroom and Library Media Program."
    3. Glen W. Cutlip. 4. 1988.  5. Libraries Unlimited.
    6. 134. 7. Yes.  8. Yes.

**4-7** Answers will vary.

**4-8** 1. 700–799. 2. 500–599. 3. 200–299. 4. 400–499. 5. 000–099.
    6. 900–999. 7. 100–199. 8. 800–899. 9. 300–399.
    10. 600–699.

**4-9** 1. E-F; 2. P; 3. B; 4. L; 5. G; 6. M; 7. N; 8. J.

**4-10** 1. 6 4 5
     2 1 3
    2. 5 3 1 4 2

**4-11** 1. Locate articles in periodicals or newspapers. 2. Short summary of an article. 3. Yes. 4. Weekly, monthly, or other regular intervals. 5. Daily or weekly 6. Database. 7. Yes. 8. No. 9. Print index. 10. Relatively new technology.

**4-12** Electronic libraries in schools = Title.
    W. E. Braunsfelsia = Author.
    *School INTERNET Review* = Magazine.
    1 = Volume.
    (4) = Issue.
    12–28 = Pages.
    D = Month.
    '95 = Year.

**4-13** Answers will vary.

**4-14** 1. "Standing Up for Music: Rapsters and Fans Defend Their Music."
    2. Aurora Times.
    3. November 12, 1995.
    4. CD Newsworld Intentional.
    5. Rap music; censorship.

6. Photo.
7. No.
8. No.

**4-15** Answers will vary.

**4-16**

**4-17** Answers will vary.

**4-18** 1. A worldwide network of large computers that are connected to each other.
2. It is like a road that gets you places.
3. Colleges and universities, research institutions, at government agencies, and private corporations.
4. Gopher.
5. Electronic mail.
6. To chat with others who have similar interests.
7. World Wide Web.
8. Words connected to other pages of web information.
9. A web browser and an account on the Internet.

**4-19** 1. Answers will vary. 2. The NASA home page. 3. National Aeronautics and Space Administration. 4. Answers will vary. 5. Brian Dunbar, Author; Jim Gass, Curator; Stephen Chambers, WebSite Designer. 6. comments@www.hq.nasa.gov

**4-20** 1. 3; 2. 16; 3. 12; 4. 9; 5. 4; 6. 14; 7. 13; 8. 5; 9. 10; 10. 7; 11. 17

**4-21** Answers will vary.

**4-22** Answers will vary.

**4-23** 1. Collect and evaluate the information.
2. Print, electronic, audio/visual, microform.
3. In a card catalog, information about an item is typed onto a card. In an online catalog, the information is entered into a computer.
4. Subject card; title card; author card.
5. By fields.
6. Ten.
7. Twenty.
8. Tell the subject of a book; give the place where it belongs on the shelf.
9. An index in electronic format.
10. The information that completely identifies a publication.
11. Identify citations related to a topic; see if the publication cited is available in the library.
12. Or; not; and.
13. An important word about the topic.
14. Worldwide network of large computers connected to each other.
15. A computer information system for your town or city.
16. com (commercial), gov (government), edu (education), org (organization).

## CHAPTER FIVE

# Using Reference Sources

## CHAPTER OBJECTIVES

1. Teach students about reference sources available in both print and electronic form.
2. Teach students strategies for locating and using reference sources.

## TITLES OF REPRODUCIBLE ACTIVITIES

## USING THE REPRODUCIBLE ACTIVITIES

After you have distributed a reproducible activity, here are some suggestions for using it. Feel free to add further information, illustrations or examples. Wherever possible, relate the activity to actual subject area assignments.

### 5-1   Identifying and Locating Reference Sources

Use the introductory text to lead a discussion about the reference section of the library. Emphasize that librarians are there to provide assistance. Discuss and show examples of frequently used types of reference sources. Point out that many reference sources are available in both print and electronic formats. Then have students answer the questions.

You may want to invite the school librarian to introduce your students to the reference sources available in the school library. This could be done at the library or in your classroom.

### 5-2   Learning about Dictionaries

Review the introductory text with students. Have students read about the five types of dictionaries. Show students any dictionaries you have in your classroom and have them identify the type for each. Then have students answer the questions.

### 5-3   Locating Print and Electronic Dictionaries

Have students use a library to complete the activity. Remind students to ask the librarian for assistance if they cannot find one or more of the types of dictionaries.

### 5-4   Information Found on a Dictionary Page

Have students read about the different types of information found on a dictionary page. Ask students to look at a page in a dictionary they use to see if all the types of information are included. Refer students to the library if they do not own a dictionary. Have students complete the activity.

### 5-5   Putting Words in Alphabetical Order

Explain to students that words in a dictionary are in alphabetical order so they can be easily found. Have students complete the activity.

### 5-6   Locating Words Quickly in the Dictionary

Explain how opening and closing guide words are used to quickly find entry words in a dictionary. Point out to students they do not have to know the meanings of the guide words. You may want to show an example of guide words from a dictionary you have in your classroom. Have students complete the activity.

### 5-7  Phonetic Respellings in the Dictionary

Review the introductory text with students. Have students use a dictionary to complete the activity. Then have students volunteer to pronounce the words using the phonetic respellings.

### 5-8  Choosing the Correct Definition

Point out that dictionaries show more than one definition of a word arranged in order of how frequently each definition of the word is used. Explain to students that before they choose a definition, they must carefully read each definition to select the definition that best fits the context in which they are using the word. Then have students complete the activity.

### 5-9  Roots of Dictionary Entry Words

Explain that entry words are listed in the dictionary as root words. Select several words from a dictionary to demonstrate how to identify the root word when a word contains a prefix, suffix, or both. Have students complete the activity.

### 5-10  Learning about Encyclopedias

Review the introductory text with students. Have students read about the five types of encyclopedias. Show students any encyclopedias you have in your classroom and have them identify the type for each. Then have students answer the questions.

### 5-11  Locating Print and Electronic Encyclopedias

Have students use a library to complete the activity. Remind them to ask the librarian for assistance if they cannot find one or more of the types of encyclopedias.

### 5-12  Using an Index in an Encyclopedia

Tell students to use the index of an encyclopedia to locate information about a topic. Point out that the volume in which they might expect to find the topic may not contain the topic or may not contain all the information about the topic. For example, a student looking for information about Disney World may not find Disney World as the title of an article in the "D" volume. However, the student might find an entry for Disney World in the index with the direction to look under "amusement parks" in the "A" volume.

Discuss the different types of information found in an encyclopedia index entry. Then have students look at the sample entry for "rap music" and answer the questions.

### 5-13  Learning about a Thesaurus

Review the introductory text with students. Have students use a thesaurus to complete the activity.

### 5-14  Practice Using Synonyms

Use the example to show students how the meaning of a sentence can be changed by substituting a synonym for one of the words. Have students complete the activity.

### 5-15  Learning about Almanacs

Review the introductory text with students. Tell them to use the index to find information in an almanac. Caution students that depending on the almanac they use, the index may be in the front, middle, or back. Have students locate almanacs in the library to complete the activity. You can use this activity as a group project or as a competition between individuals and/or groups. Later, lead a discussion about the way students located information and what they learned about using almanacs.

### 5-16  Learning about Atlases

Have students read about the five types of atlases. Show students any atlases you have in your classroom and have them identify the type for each. Then have students answer the questions.

### 5-17  Locating Print and Electronic Atlases

Have students use a library to complete the activity. Remind students to ask the librarian for assistance if they cannot find one or more of the types of atlases.

### 5-18 Other Types of Reference Sources

Review the descriptions of these other reference sources with students. Lead a discussion about when students might want to consult these other types of reference sources. Then have students answer the questions.

### 5-19 Chapter Five Mastery Assessment

Have students complete this assessment at any point you believe they have learned about reference sources and how and when to use them. Review the results of the assessment with the students. Provide additional instruction as necessary.

# Identifying and Locating Reference Sources

Reference sources are used to find information on a topic quickly. The most frequently used reference sources are encyclopedias, dictionaries, almanacs, atlases, and indexes to articles. Reference sources are shelved in the reference section of the library. There is usually a reference desk staffed by a librarian to help you identify and locate reference sources.

1. What are reference sources?

2. What are the most frequently used reference sources?

3. Who can help you locate reference sources?

Many reference sources are available on CD ROM. Some CD ROM reference sources are multimedia. They are called multimedia because they contain images, sound, video and animation. Other CD ROM reference sources are text only. This means they do not include pictures, maps, or other illustrations.

4. What are multimedia reference sources?

5. What are text-only CD ROM reference sources?

Dictionaries are reference books that provide information about words. Dictionaries help you pronounce a word, discover its meaning, and learn how it is spelled. Dictionaries are made up of entries. An entry is a word, abbreviation, prefix, suffix, or word part that is listed and defined in the dictionary. Dictionaries are available in print and electronic form.

There are five basic types of dictionaries. Each has its own value. Knowing about the different types will help you decide when to use each.

**Unabridged Dictionaries.**   **Unabridged** means not condensed or shortened. Unabridged dictionaries attempt to include all words currently in use in a language. An example of an unabridged dictionary is the *Random House Dictionary of the English Language.*

**Abridged Dictionaries.**   **Abridged** means shortened by the omission of something. Abridged dictionaries are shortened forms of unabridged dictionaries. Abridged dictionaries omit words that are not frequently used. They are smaller, lighter, and less expensive than abridged dictionaries. An example of an abridged dictionary is the *American Heritage Dictionary.*

**Etymological Dictionaries.**   **Etymology** is the history of words. Etymological dictionaries tell the history of words and explain how their meaning has changed over time. Etymological dictionaries can be one or more volumes. An example of an etymological dictionary is the *Oxford English Dictionary.*

**Slang Dictionaries.**   **Slang** is used mostly for casual speech. An example of slang is "Cool it." The meaning of this slang expression is "Calm down." An example of a slang dictionary is the *New Dictionary of American Slang.*

**Subject Dictionaries.**   Special dictionaries are found for many **subjects,** such as medicine, psychology, art, music, business, science, and technology. An unabridged dictionary will probably have a definition for a technical word in a given subject. However, if a special dictionary exists for that subject, a longer or more complete definition will be found in the subject dictionary. An example of a subject dictionary is *Stedman's Medical Dictionary.*

1. Where should you look to find the most complete definition of a technical word?

2. Where can you look to find words used in casual speech?

3. What kind of dictionary includes almost every word that people use today?

4. Where would you find the meaning of a word as it was used in the 1700s?

5. What are shortened dictionaries called?

Dictionaries are found in print or electronic form. Find an example of each of the following types of dictionaries. Write its title and call number. Check (✔) Dewey Decimal (DD) or Library of Congress (LC) to show the classification system of the call number. Then check Print or Electronic to show the format of the dictionary.

### Unabridged Dictionary

Title _____     Call number _____

DD _____ LC _____           Print _____ Electronic _____

### Abridged Dictionary

Title _____     Call number _____

DD _____ LC _____           Print _____ Electronic _____

### Etymological Dictionary

Title _____     Call number _____

DD _____ LC _____           Print _____ Electronic _____

### Slang Dictionary

Title _____     Call number _____

DD _____ LC _____           Print _____ Electronic _____

### Subject Dictionary

Title _____     Call number _____

DD _____ LC _____           Print _____ Electronic _____

Read about the types of information found on a dictionary page.

1. *Guide words:* There are two guide words at the top of every dictionary page. The first guide word is called the *opening guide word* and tells the first word on the page. The second guide word is called the *closing guide word* and tells the last word on the page.

2. *Entry words:* These are the words listed and defined on the dictionary page. They appear in darker or bolder type on the dictionary page.

3. *Phonetic respelling:* After each entry word you will see a respelling for that entry. The respelling often uses different letters and symbols to show you how to pronounce the word. If you do not know what the letters or symbols mean, look at the *short pronunciation key* found at the bottom of every right-hand page.

4. *Part of speech:* Usually following the respelling you will find an abbreviation that tells the part of speech of the entry. Here are the abbreviations for the common parts of speech:

   | | |
   |---|---|
   | n = noun | pron = pronoun |
   | v = verb | adv = adverb |
   | adj = adjective | prep = preposition |

5. *Definitions:* The definitions for each entry word are presented. The definitions are numbered to show the order of their common use. The most commonly used definition appears first, following the number 1. The next most common definition is numbered 2, and so on.

6. *Variants of the word:* Different forms of the word may also be presented as part of the entry. For example, for the word *define* you may also find the variants *defined* and *defining.*

7. *Origin or etymology:* In some dictionaries you will also find information that tells you where the word came from. For example, the letter *G* might be used to show that the word came from the Greek language, or *L* to show that it has a Latin origin.

8. *Correct usage in a sentence:* Sometimes a sentence containing the entry word is provided. The sentence shows how the word is used in a sentence. For example, to illustrate the meaning of the word *enforce,* the following sentence might be provided:

   A police officer must *enforce* the law.

9. *Synonym or antonym:* Sometimes following the abbreviation *syn* a synonym for the entry word is provided. Sometimes following *ant* an antonym is provided.

10. *Illustration:* Sometimes drawings, pictures, or other types of visuals are presented to illustrate the word.

11. *Short pronunciation key:* This key to the pronunciation of words is usually found at the bottom of every right-hand page. The short pronunciation key contains letters, symbols, and words that will help you pronounce entries you do not know how to say. If the short pronunciation key does not help you pronounce an entry, then look at the long pronunciation key located in the front of your dictionary.

Identify each type of information by placing a number in the box near the information provided in the dictionary entry and from the bottom of a dictionary page.

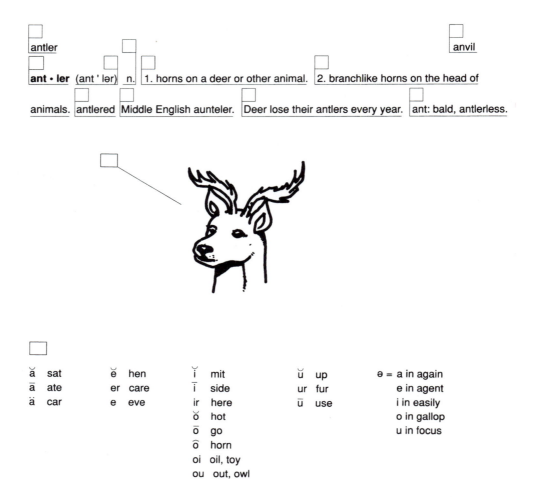

antler
□
□
anvil

**ant · ler** (ant ' lər)  n.  1. horns on a deer or other animal.  2. branchlike horns on the head of animals.  antlered  Middle English aunteler.  Deer lose their antlers every year.  ant: bald, antlerless.

| | | |
|---|---|---|
| ă sat | ĕ hen | ĭ mit |
| ā ate | er care | ī side |
| ä car | e eve | ir here |

| | |
|---|---|
| ŭ up | ə = a in again |
| ur fur | e in agent |
| ū use | i in easily |
| | o in gallop |
| | u in focus |

ŏ hot
ō go
ô horn
oi oil, toy
ou out, owl

Entry words in a dictionary are listed in alphabetical order. Here are sets of words as they might appear on a dictionary page. Arrange each set in alphabetical order.

1. humid
   humble
   humor
   humility

2. pond
   pound
   poodle
   ponder

3. murder
   murky
   mumps
   municipal

4. individual
   indulge
   indifferent
   inert

5. casual
   case
   carton
   cash

6. sorrel
   sorrow
   sorcery
   sore

7. aspect
   assign
   associate
   assortment

8. mental
   melon
   melting
   memory

You will find a pair of guide words at the top of each page in a dictionary. The first is called an **opening guide word** and is the first word listed and defined on that dictionary page. The second is called the **closing guide word** and is the last word listed and defined on that page. All the entry words that appear on that dictionary page are in alphabetical order, starting with the opening guide word and ending with the closing guide word.

Here are three sets of words. For each word in a set, write the letter that shows the guide words for the page where you would find it.

| Word to Find | Opening Guide Word | Closing Guide Word |
|---|---|---|
| **SET ONE** | | |
| 1. _____ term | a. tendency | tenor |
| 2. _____ test | b. terrorism | testy |
| 3. _____ tennis | c. tercentenary | termite |
| **SET TWO** | | |
| 1. _____ neglect | a. neighborhood | neology |
| 2. _____ necessary | b. negative | neighbor |
| 3. _____ neither | c. near | neck |
| **SET THREE** | | |
| 1. _____ volume | a. volcano | voluntary |
| 2. _____ vulgar | b. volunteer | voucher |
| 3. _____ vote | c. vouchsafe | vulture |

**Phonetic** (fe net′ ik) **respellings** are used in a dictionary to help you say a word. The phonetic respelling follows the entry word on the dictionary page. When you do not know how to pronounce a word, use the phonetic respelling along with the short pronunciation key to pronounce the word. Usually the short pronunciation key is found at the bottom of each page in the dictionary. If you still cannot pronounce the word, try using the phonetic respelling along with the long pronunciation key, which will be found at the front of the dictionary.

Use your dictionary to find the phonetic respelling for each of the following words. Copy the phonetic respelling for each word. Use the phonetic respelling and either the short or long pronunciation key found in your dictionary to pronounce each word.

eventually     _____

plumber     _____

familiar     _____

sphere     _____

pneumatic     _____

goody     _____

jargon     _____

mire     _____

intuition     _____

mosaic     _____

nutmeat     _____

nutmeg     _____

nutrition     _____

# Choosing the Correct Definition

Many words in the English language have more than one meaning. This is why many entry words are followed by more than one definition. Each definition is numbered to separate it from the others. The first definition is the most commonly used meaning of the word, and the last definition is the least commonly used.

Read each sentence and think about what the highlighted word means in the sentence. Then read the definitions for the highlighted word. Use the meaning of the sentence to help you decide which definition best fits the sentence. Write the definition that best fits the meaning of the sentence.

1. The *palm* broke as I pulled on the oar.

    **palm** (päm) n.   1. bottom part of hand.   2. part of animal forefoot.   3. part of a glove.   4. blade of an oar.   5. linear measure 7–10 inches.   6. to conceal.   7. to pick up stealthily.

    _____

2. The policewoman gave the driver a *summons* for driving through the red light.

    **summons** (sum' ənz) n.   1. a call to attend a meeting.   2. an official order to appear in court.   3. a traffic ticket.

    _____

3. Before leaving for the trip we placed our *dunnage* in the trunk of the car.

    **dunnage** (dun' ij) n.   1. baggage or personal items.   2. loose material wedged between objects.   3. a cover.

    _____

4. Mary went on an *odyssey* around the world.

    **odyssey** (od' i sē) n.   1. a trip characterized by wandering.   2. poem attributed to Homer.   3. a dream.

    _____

5. Sir Henry is the *Grand* Duke of Windsor.

    **grand** (grand) adj.   1. standing out in size and beauty.   2. costly.   3. higher in rank than others.   4. amount of money.

    _____

Sometimes you cannot find a word in the dictionary because the word you are looking for has a prefix, a suffix, or both a prefix and a suffix. To find the word you want, you must first remove the prefix, suffix, or both. What remains is called the **root word.** Then you can look for the root word in the dictionary. Write the root word for each of the following:

1. unafraid

2. repainting

3. fairest

4. nonabrasive

5. transportable

6. reappear

Sometimes the root word ends in *e* and the *e* is dropped when adding a suffix that begins with a vowel. For example: **bike + ing = biking, trade + ed = traded.** When this is the case, you must remember to add the *e* when writing the root word. Write the root word for each of the following:

7. smiling

8. graced

9. believable

10. sensible

11. cascaded

12. likable

13. trading

14. choosing

Sometimes words that end in a single consonant have that consonant doubled before adding a suffix that begins with a vowel. For example: **run + ing = running, bat + er = batter.** When this is the case, you must remember to drop both the second consonant and the suffix when writing the root word. Write the root word for each of the following:

15. jogging

16. mobbed

17. tripped

18. hugged

19. winner

20. sledding

21. putting

22. shipping

An encyclopedia contains articles on a variety of subjects written by experts. The articles are arranged in alphabetical order by topic. There are five basic types of encyclopedias. Each has its own value. Knowing about the different types will help you decide when to use each one.

**General encyclopedias** include overview articles on a wide range of topics. The articles are arranged alphabetically in a set of volumes. Illustrations are also included. The last volume in the set is the index. Information is kept up-to-date with articles published in yearbooks or supplements. An example of a general encyclopedia is the *Encyclopedia Americana*.

**Single-volume encyclopedias** include short articles arranged in alphabetical order. There is no index or table of contents. An example of a single volume encyclopedia is the *Random House Encyclopedia*.

**Encyclopedias for children and young adults** are general encyclopedias that are written and designed for a specific age group. There are many illustrations and study aids and they are easier to read than other encyclopedias. An example of an encyclopedia for children and young adults is the *World Book Encyclopedia*.

**Foreign language encyclopedias** are found in three forms:

- Encyclopedias written from the perspective of another country and published in the language of that country such as the *Enzyklopadie Brockhaus*.
- Encyclopedias written from the perspective of another country but translated into English such as *Great Soviet Encyclopedia*.
- Encyclopedias published in the United States but in a foreign language such as *Chinese Language Concise Encyclopaedia Britannica*.

**Subject encyclopedias** are found for many subjects, such as medicine, psychology, art, music, business, science, and technology. The articles are longer, more complete, and more technical than those found in general encyclopedias. An example of a subject encyclopedia is the *McGraw-Hill Encyclopedia of Science and Technology*.

1. When would you look up your topic in a subject encyclopedia?

2. What type of encyclopedia would have extensive illustrations?

3. What type of encyclopedia contains many volumes and includes articles on a wide variety of topics?

4. What is not included with a single-volume encyclopedia?

5. What are the three forms of foreign language encyclopedias?

Encyclopedias are found in print or electronic form. Find an example of each of the following types of encyclopedias. Write its title and call number. Check (✔) Dewey Decimal (DD) or Library of Congress (LC) to show the classification system of the call number. Then check Print or Electronic to show the format of the encyclopedia.

### General Encyclopedia

Title _____                  Call number _____

DD _____  LC _____                       Print _____  Electronic _____


### Single-Volume Encyclopedia

Title _____                  Call number _____

DD _____  LC _____                       Print _____  Electronic _____


### Encyclopedia for Children and Young Adults

Title _____                  Call number _____

DD _____  LC _____                       Print _____  Electronic _____


### Foreign Language Encyclopedia

Title _____                  Call number _____

DD _____  LC _____                       Print _____  Electronic _____


### Subject Encyclopedia

Title _____                  Call number _____

DD _____  LC _____                       Print _____  Electronic _____

When you look for information in an encyclopedia, begin by selecting a keyword from your topic to look up in the index. Select another keyword if you cannot find your first keyword. For example, using the keyword *rap* from the topic "Rap music in America," you might find the following index entry.

Study the sample index entry and answer the questions.

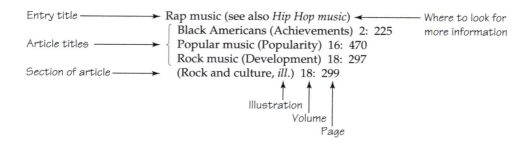

1. In what articles will you find information about the topic?

2. In the article "Black Americans," under what section will you find information about the topic?

3. In what volume and on what page will you find the information about the popularity of rap music?

4. In what volume and on what page will you find an illustration relating to rap music?

5. Where would you look for more information about the topic?

A **thesaurus** (thi sor´ əs) contains synonyms for commonly used words. The entry words are organized in alphabetical order. Following each entry word is its part of speech and a list of synonyms.

You can use a thesaurus to select words that help you precisely express your ideas when you are writing. Read the following to see how different synonyms change the meaning of the sentence.

> The bank *took* control of the company.
> The bank *grabbed* control of the company.
> The bank *seized* control of the company.

A **thesaurus** is different from a **dictionary.** A thesaurus contains a large number of synonyms for each entry word. It also gives the part of speech for each synonym. Unlike a dictionary, it does not contain phonetic respellings, definitions, variants of the word, origins of the word, correct usage in sentences, antonyms, or illustrations. A thesaurus contains many more synonyms for commonly used words than a dictionary does. However, a dictionary contains a greater variety of information on each word.

Look at the sample entry for the word *raw* found in a thesaurus. It shows the entry word, the part of speech, and a number of synonyms that can be used in place of the entry word.

> **raw**   adj.   uncooked, crude, inexperienced, rude, coarse, obscene

For each of the following sentences, use a thesaurus to find a synonym you can use in place of the highlighted word. Select the synonym that most precisely expresses the idea of the sentence. Write the synonym next to the sentence.

1. John will *gain* from the advice given to him.

2. Man has loved *animals* since the *start* of time.

3. Jane had a *fantastic* time at the rock concert.

4. It is important for teachers to *excite* their students to learn.

5. "Be careful or you will *tumble!*" His mother shouted.

6. Luis went to the grocery store to *obtain* a carton of milk.

7. Paula looked throughout the department store for new *garb* to wear to school.

8. The entire class *moaned* when the test was announced.

9. He was *undecided* about going to the party.

10. Sam was excited about moving into his new *dwelling*.

Read the following two sentences.

Did you see Joe *eat* the food?
Did you see Tom *devour* the food?

Notice how using the synonym *devour* instead of *eat* in the second sentence changes the meaning of the sentence. Although both *eat* and *devour* have the same general meaning, each has its own specific meaning. The word *eat* suggests consuming food in a slow and orderly manner using a knife and fork. The word *devour* suggests consuming food rapidly using one's hands to rip the food into pieces. Bill eats his food. Joe devours his food. Who would you bring home for dinner?

Read the following pairs of sentences. The first sentence has a highlighted word. In the second sentence that word has been replaced with a synonym found in a thesaurus. Read the two sentences and explain how the meaning of the sentence has been changed. You may need to go to a dictionary to look up the definitions of the words.

1. Mary is an *attractive* girl.
   Mary is a *gorgeous* girl.

   _____

2. *Write* your name on this page.
   *Scribble* your name on this page.

   _____

3. He found his new classmate to be *unfriendly*.
   He found his new classmates to be *hostile*.

   _____

4. Betty did her homework in a *careless* manner.
   Betty did her homework in a *listless* manner.

   _____

5. I have an *obsolete* car in my garage.
   I have an *antique* car in my garage.

   _____

6. She was *angry* when she saw her grade.
   She was *furious* when she saw her grade.

   _____

An **almanac** is a single-volume reference book containing facts, data, tables, charts, lists, and other methods of organizing useful information. Almanacs provide information about a wide range of topics. Some of the most frequently used almanacs are:

Information Please Almanac
New York Public Library Desk Reference
Universal Almanac
Whitaker's Almanack
World Almanac and Book of Facts

Use one of the almanacs listed above or any other almanac to answer the questions that follow. For each question, write the answer to the question and the title of the almanac containing the information needed to answer the question. Also include the page number(s) where the information appears in the almanac.

1. What are the names of the volcanoes in Sicily?

2. What is the name of the U.S. presidential candidate who lost the election to George Bush in 1988?

3. How many divorces were there in the United States in 1990 as compared to 1900?

4. What is the highest temperature ever recorded in the state of California?

5. What were three world headline news stories in 1959?

6. Who was the governor of Wisconsin in 1995?

7. Who invented the electric razor?

# Learning about Atlases

An **atlas** is a collection of maps. There are four basic types of atlases. Each has its own value. Knowing about the different types will help you decide when to use each.

**General World Atlas.** General world atlases contain maps showing physical and political features of countries throughout the world. Most general world atlases include sections of maps on specific topics such as climate, population, and health. An example of a general atlas is the *Hammond Atlas of the World.* Some general atlases are available in electronic form. For example, *Global Explorer* is a general atlas available on CD ROM.

**Historical Atlas.** Historical atlases contain maps that portray an event or show how something developed or changed over a period of time. Historical atlases include information about topics such as changes in borders, military campaigns, exploration, and culture. An historical atlas usually has the word *history* or *historical* in its title. An example of an historical atlas is the *Times Atlas of World History.*

**Subject Atlas.** Subject atlases contain maps related to a specific place, such as the *National Atlas of Canada,* or about a topic, such as the *Atlas of the Christian Church.*

**Road Atlas.** Road atlases contain maps that show major highways and secondary roads for a geographical area. An example of a road atlas is the *Rand McNally Road Atlas.*

1. What is an atlas?

2. What type of atlas would you use to find political maps of countries all over the world?

3. What type of atlas would you use to find maps depicting famous battles in history?

4. What is a subject atlas?

5. What type of atlas would you use to plan a long automobile trip?

6. Do you have an atlas at home? If yes, what is its title?

Atlases are found in print or electronic form. Find an example of each of the following types of atlases. Write its title and call number. Check (✔) Dewey Decimal (DD) or Library of Congress (LC) to show the classification system of the call number. Then check Print or Electronic to show the format of the atlas.

### General Atlas

Title _____   Call number _____

DD _____   LC _____   Print _____   Electronic _____

### Historical Atlas

Title _____   Call number _____

DD _____   LC _____   Print _____   Electronic _____

### Subject Atlas

Title _____   Call number _____

DD _____   LC _____   Print _____   Electronic _____

### Road Atlas

Title _____   Call number _____

DD _____   LC _____   Print _____   Electronic _____

# Other Types of Reference Sources  5-18

Here are additional reference sources you should know about.

**Biographical.** Biographical sources provide concise background information about the lives and accomplishments of famous people, living or dead. Use these sources if you do not need or cannot find an entire book about a person.

Examples:　Dictionary of Literary Biography　Webster's Biographical Dictionary
　　　　　　Contemporary Authors　　　　　Current Biography
　　　　　　Dictionary of Scientific Biography　Biography Index

**Literary Criticism.** Literary criticism sources provide biographical information about writers, a list of their works, and excerpts from articles and books about their works. You can find literary criticism sources for all categories of literature, such as plays, poetry, short stories, and novels.

Examples:　Contemporary Literary Criticism　Short Story Criticism
　　　　　　Poetry Criticism　　　　　　　Nineteenth Century Literary Criticism

**Chronology.** A chronology is a reference book that presents information organized by date. Chronologies may cover events over a long period of time, such as hundreds of years, or as short a period as one year. Some chronologies cover all subjects while others cover specific subjects.

Examples:　People's Chronology　　Timetables of Technology

**Weekly Compilation of News Stories.** These sources provide short summaries of national and international news for a given week. Because they are updated weekly, they provide very current information.

Examples:　Facts on File　　Keesing's Contemporary Archives

**Opposing Viewpoints.** These sources identify currently controversial issues and present all viewpoints. They are particularly useful for selecting a topic for a paper.

Examples:　CQ Researcher　　Opposing Viewpoints

From the reference sources described in this activity, write the type you would use to do the following:

1.  Identify important events that occurred in Europe last week.

2.  Find a critical essay about a play.

3.  Identify important events that occurred in 1965.

4.  Locate arguments for and against the death penalty.

5.  Learn about a famous German scientist.

6.  Learn about the theme of a novel.

7.  Identify five famous female athletes.

8.  Prepare for a debate about gun control.

9.  Find a current news story about unemployment.

10. Learn about the life and works of a contemporary Caribbean writer.

See what you have learned about using reference sources.

**1.** What are the five most frequently used types of reference sources?

**2.** What are the five basic types of dictionaries?

**3.** What is an unabridged dictionary?

**4.** What are phonetic respellings?

**5.** What are the five basic types of encyclopedias?

**6.** What is an important difference between a general encyclopedia and a subject encyclopedia?

**7.** What information about an article will you find in the index to an encyclopedia?

**8.** What is a thesaurus?

**9.** What is an almanac?

**10.** What are the four basic types of atlases?

**11.** What kind of information is found in literary criticism sources?

**5-1** 1. Sources used to quickly find information on a topic. 2. Encyclopedias, dictionaries, almanacs, atlases, and indexes to articles. 3. Librarian. 4. CD ROM sources that contain images, sound, video, and animation. 5. CD ROM sources that do not include pictures, maps, or other illustrations.

**5-2** 1. Subject dictionary. 2. Slang dictionary. 3. Unabridged dictionary. 4. Etymological dictionary. 5. Abridged dictionary.

**5-3** Answers will vary.

**5-4**

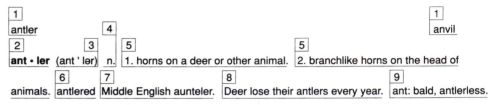

| 1 antler | | | | | 1 anvil |
|----------|--|--|--|--|---------|

| 2 **ant · ler** (ant ' ler) n. | 3 | 5 1. horns on a deer or other animal. | 5 2. branchlike horns on the head of |
|--|--|--|--|

| 6 animals. | 7 antlered | Middle English aunteler. | 8 Deer lose their antlers every year. | 9 ant: bald, antlerless. |
|--|--|--|--|--|

10

11

| ă | sat | ĕ | hen | i | mit | u | up | ə = a in again |
|---|-----|---|-----|---|-----|---|-----|----------------|
| ā | ate | er | care | ī | side | ur | fur | e in agent |
| ä | car | e | eve | ir | here | ū | use | i in easily |
| | | | | ŏ | hot | | | o in gallop |
| | | | | ō | go | | | u in focus |
| | | | | ô | horn | | | |
| | | | | oi | oil, toy | | | |
| | | | | ou | out, owl | | | |

FIG *PAGE 216*
SIZE____*80*___%
ASTERISK GROUP

**5-5** 1. humble, humid, humility, humor 2. pond, ponder, poodle, pound 3. mumps, municipal, murder, murky 4. indifferent, individual, indulge, inert 5. carton, case, cash, casual 6. sorcery, sore, sorrel, sorrow 7. aspect, assign, associate, assortment 8. melon, melting, memory, mental

**5-6** Set One. 1. C. 2. B. 3. A.  Set Two. 1. B. 2. C. 3. A. Set Three. 1. A. 2. C. 3. B.

**5-7** Answers will vary with the dictionary used by each student.

**5-8** 1. blade of an oar. 2. a traffic ticket. 3. baggage or personal items. 4. a trip characterized by wandering. 5. higher in rank than others.

**5-9** 1. afraid. 2. paint. 3. fair. 4. abrasive. 5. transport. 6. appear. 7. smile. 8. grace. 9. believe. 10. sense. 11. cascade. 12. like. 13. trade. 14. choose. 15. jog. 16. mob. 17. trip. 18. hug. 19. win. 20. sled. 21. put. 22. ship.

**5-10** 1. When you want to find articles that are longer, more complete, and more technical than those found in general encyclopedias.
2. Encyclopedias for children and young adults.
3. General encyclopedias
4. Index or table of contents
5. Encyclopedias written from the perspective of another country and published in the language of that country; encyclopedias written from the perspective of another country but translated into English; encyclopedias published in the United States but in a foreign language.

**5-11** Answers will vary.

**5-12** 1. Black Americans; Popular Music; Rock Music. 2. Achievements. 3. Volume 16, page 470. 4. Volume 18, page 299. 5. Hip Hop music.

**5-13** Answers will vary.

**5-14** 1. *Gorgeous* shows more beauty. 2. *Scribble* means the writing is not neat. 3. *Hostile* means the classmates were dangerous. 4. *Listless* means the homework was done with little effort. 5. *Antique* shows the car is old and of some value. 6. *Furious* shows rage and possible violence.

**5-15** Answers will vary.

**5-16** 1. A collection of maps. 2. General world atlas. 3. Historical atlas. 4. Contains maps related to a specific place or topic. 5. Road atlas. 6. Answers will vary.

**5-17** Answers will vary.

**5-18** 1. Weekly compilation of news stories. 2. Literary criticism. 3. Chronology. 4. Opposing viewpoints. 5. Biographical. 6. Literary criticism. 7. Biographical. 8. Opposing viewpoints. 9. Weekly compilation of news stories. 10. Literary criticism or biographical.

**5-19**  1. Encyclopedias, dictionaries, almanacs, atlases, and indexes to articles.
2. Unabridged, abridged, etymological, slang, subject.
3. Includes all words currently in use in a language.
4. Respellings used in dictionaries to help you say a word.
5. General, single volume, encyclopedia for children and young adults, foreign language, and subject.
6. General encyclopedias have overview articles on topics, while subject encyclopedias articles that are longer, more complete, and more technical.
7. Entry title, article title, section(s) of articles, volume, page number(s), illustrated or not, where to look for more information.
8. Contains synonyms for commonly used words.
9. Single volume reference book that contains facts, data, tables, charts, lists, and other methods of organizing useful information.
10. General world, historical, subject, road.
11. Biographical information about writers, a list of their works, excerpts from articles and books about their works.

## CHAPTER SIX

# Interpreting Visual Aids

## CHAPTER OBJECTIVES

1. Teach students the different visual aids found in textbooks and other sources of information.
2. Teach students to interpret visual aids.

## TITLES OF REPRODUCIBLE ACTIVITIES

## USING THE REPRODUCIBLE ACTIVITIES

After you have distributed a reproducible activity, here are suggestions for its use. Feel free to add further information, illustrations, or examples. Wherever possible, relate the activity to actual subject area assignments.

### 6-1 Political Map

Tell students they will be learning about political, physical, road, weather, and data maps. This activity introduces the political map. The political map shown shows the boundaries of countries within a geographical region. Have students use the political map of Central America to answer the questions.

### 6-2 Another Political Map

Bring out that some political maps show political divisions within a country. Just like the United States is divided into states and territories, Canada is divided into provinces and territories. Have students use the political map of Canada to answer the questions.

### 6-3 Physical Map

Point out that physical maps show the features of the earth's surface such as mountains, highlands, plateaus, deserts, and major bodies of water. Define any unknown features. Have students use the physical map of South America to answer the questions.

### 6-4 Road Map

Bring out that road maps are used to get from one place to another when traveling over roadways. Have students use the road map to answer the questions.

### 6-5 Weather Map for Current Conditions

Tell students they will find weather maps in newspapers and on television news programs. Bring out that most weather maps describe weather conditions for a specific day. Have students use the weather map to answer the questions.

### 6-6 Outlook Weather Map

Help students understand that weather maps can also be used to forecast future weather. Have students use the outlook weather map to answer the questions.

### 6-7  Data Map

Bring out that maps can also be used to provide data along with information to explain conditions for a geographical area. Have students use the data map showing U.S. population growth to answer the questions.

### 6-8  Pictograph

Tell students they will be learning about pictographs, pie or circle graphs, bar graphs, and line graphs. This activity introduces the pictograph. Bring out that a pictograph uses pictures to provide information. Have students use the pictograph showing the world's ten largest cities to answer the questions.

### 6-9  Pie or Circle Graph

Remind students that a pie graph is sometimes called a circle graph. Bring out that pie or circle graphs show the relationship between parts of something and the whole (100%). Then have students use the pie graph showing U.S. merchandise exports to answer the questions.

### 6-10  Bar Graph

Point out that the bars are vertical on these graphs depicting hourly wages by level of education. Explain how information is displayed on bar graphs. Have students use the bar graphs to answer the questions.

### 6-11  Another Form of a Bar Graph

Tell students that on some bar graphs the bars are presented horizontally rather than vertically. Have students use the bar graph to answer the questions.

### 6-12  Line Graph

Tell students that a line graph is the most appropriate graph for showing trends over a period of time. You may need to explain the meaning of the terms *outlays* (spending), *receipts* (income), and *deficit* (more spending than income). Have students use the line graph to answer the questions.

### 6-13 Diagram

Lead students to understand that diagrams are used to show something and its parts. Remind students that in some diagrams the parts are labeled while in others the parts are identified in a key. Have students use the diagram to answer the questions.

### 6-14 Table

Review the contents of the table with the students. Bring out that it would be difficult to present this information in writing and that a table makes the information easier to understand. Have students use the table to answer the questions.

### 6-15 Organizational Chart

Tell students that large organizations typically have a chart that shows how they are organized. Direct students to the organizational chart of the U.S. government. Have students use the organizational chart to answer the questions.

### 6-16 Flow Chart

Bring out that a flow chart is an effective tool for showing how something works or happens. Explain that symbols and arrows are used to show the content and flow of a process. Have students use the flow chart to answer the questions.

### 6-17 Chapter Six Mastery Assessment

Have students complete this assessment at any point you believe they have learned about visual aids and how to interpret them. Review the results of the assessment with the students. Provide additional instruction as necessary.

# Political Map

A **political map** shows the boundaries of countries, subdivisions such as states or provinces, and the location of cities and towns. Look at the political map of Central America. This region is bordered on the north by Mexico and on the south by Colombia. Lines are used on the map to show the boundaries of the countries that make up Central America. * are used to show capitals and • to show cities.

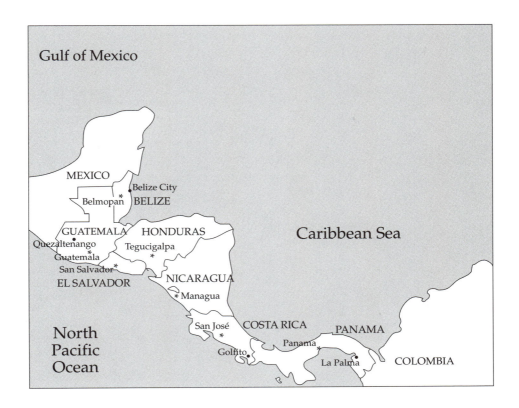

Use the political map of Central America to answer these questions:

1. How many countries make up Central America?

2. What are their names?

3. Which two countries border Mexico?

4. Which country borders Colombia?

5. What is the capital of Costa Rica?

6. In which country will you find a city named Managua?

7. Which city is closer to Mexico—Tegucigalpa or Belmopan?

A **political map of a country** is used to show the subdivisions within a country. Often capitals and major cities are also shown. Look at the political map of Canada and you will see the ten provinces and two territories that form this country. You will also see some capital cities.

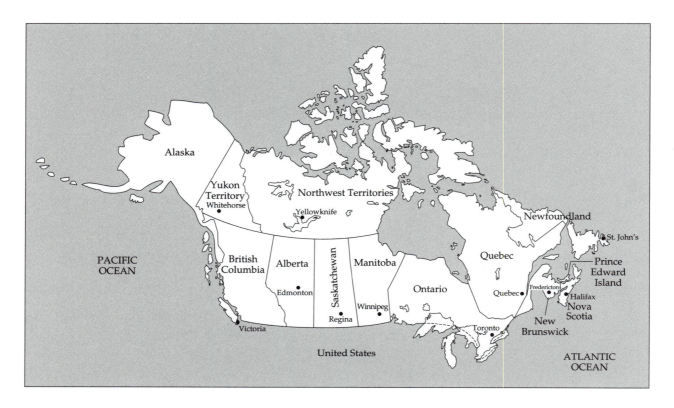

Use the political map of Canada to answer these questions:

1. How many provinces are there?

2. Name them.

3. How many territories are there?

4. Name them.

5. Which territory borders Alaska?

6. What is its capital?

7. What is the name of the largest province?

# Physical Map

A **physical map** shows the features of earth's surface, such as mountains, highlands, plateaus, deserts, and major bodies of water. Look at the physical map of the continent of South America. Notice how the features are shown. Notice, too, that no political boundaries are shown on a physical map.

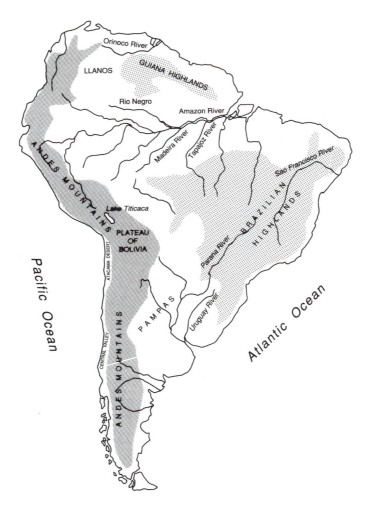

Use the physical map of South America to complete the following:

1. Write the name of the mountains.

2. Write the names of the highlands.

3. Write the name of a plateau.

4. The Amazon, Rio Negro, and Madeira are all _____ ?

5. Name the lake found on the map.

6. What do the shaded areas show on this map?

**Road maps** show the major highways and secondary roads in a geographical area. They are used to decide which highways and roads can be traveled to get from one place to another. In the following road map major highways are shown using dark lines and secondary roads using light lines. Both highways and roads are identified by numbers.

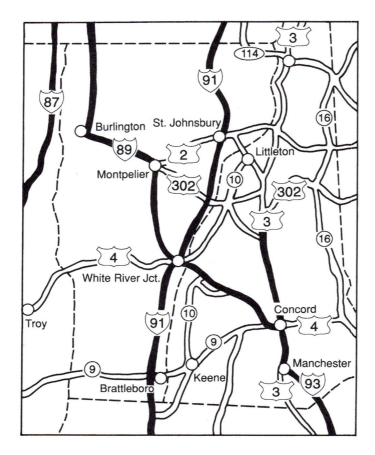

Use the road map to answer these questions:

1. Write the numbers of the highways.

2. Which two cities are located on Highway 89?

3. To travel from Manchester to Concord, what highway should be taken?

4. What road will get you to Troy?

5. Which highway goes through White River Jct.?

6. At what junction will you find St. Johnsbury?

7. Will Highway 89 take you to Keene?

One use of a **weather map** is to provide information about current weather conditions. A weather map and its symbols tell about current weather conditions in a geographical area. Here is a weather map showing the weather for one day.

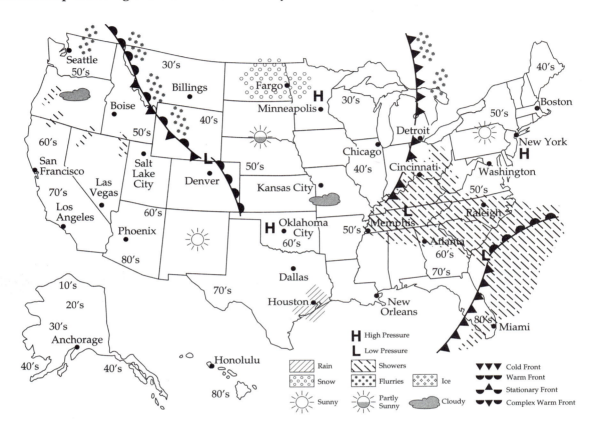

Use the United States weather map and symbols to answer the questions about weather conditions on the day the map was published.

1. Draw the symbols used to show rain, sunny weather, low pressure, and a warm front.

2. What will the weather be like in Seattle?

3. Near what cities will it snow?

4. Near what two cities will you find the warmest temperatures?

5. What will the weather be like in Houston?

6. What are the pressure conditions near Oklahoma City? Near Denver?

7. From an examination of weather fronts, what will happen to the temperature in southern Florida? In the Atlanta and Raleigh areas? Near Boise and Billings?

Another use of a weather map is to forecast future weather conditions. Some weather maps are used to forecast the next day's weather and others to forecast weather for the next several days, the next week, the next month, or even for a year. Look at the outlook weather map which was published on a Sunday, with forecasts for the next several days.

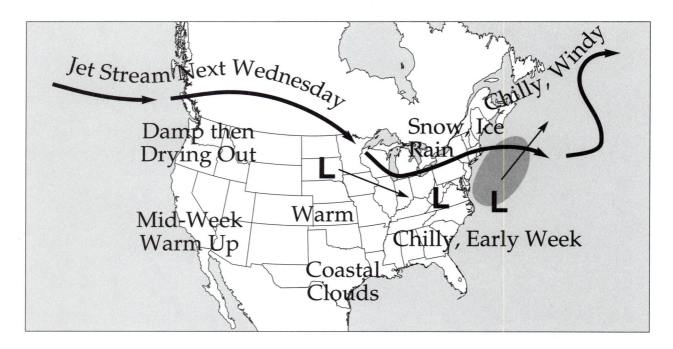

Use the outlook weather map to answer the questions.

1. In which direction is the jet stream moving across the United States?

2. What is the outlook for the northwestern United States?

3. In which part of the country will the weather be chilly on Monday and Tuesday?

4. In which part of the country will conditions be most favorable for skiing?

5. What type of weather can you expect for a midweek outdoor picnic in southern California?

6. What type of weather can you expect at Texas beaches along the Gulf of Mexico?

# Data Map

A **data map** is used to show information and data about something for a geographical region. The following data map shows the changes in population across the United States for the period 1960–1990.

**U.S. Population Growth: 1960-1990**

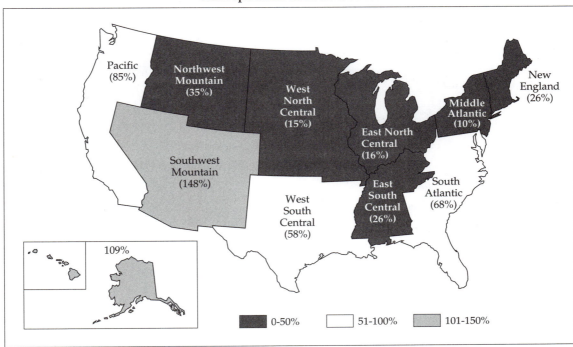

*Source:* U.S. government.

Use the map and map legend to answer the questions. For some questions you may need to refer to a political map of the United States.

1. Which section of the United States had the most rapid growth in population over the past 30 years?

2. What states are in this section?

3. Which section has had the slowest growth?

4. What was the growth rate in Hawaii and Alaska?

5. Which section has had the higher population growth rate?

   • East North Central or West North Central?

   • South Atlantic or West South Central?

   • New England or Pacific?

A **pictograph** is a type of graph in which pictures are used to provide information. A pictograph has a title that tells what it shows. It also has a key that tells what a picture stands for and the amount it represents. Sometimes only a part of a picture is shown to represent a fraction of the amount the picture stands for.

**The World's Ten Largest Cities**

| Rank | City | Country | Population (in millions) |
|------|------|---------|--------------------------|
| 1 | Tokyo-Yokohama | Japan | 🚹🚹🚹🚹🚹🚹🚹🚹🚹🚹🚹🚹🚹 |
| 2 | Mexico | Mexico | 🚹🚹🚹🚹🚹🚹🚹🚹🚹🚹🚹 |
| 3 | São Paulo | Brazil | 🚹🚹🚹🚹🚹🚹🚹🚹🚹🚹 |
| 4 | Seoul | South Korea | 🚹🚹🚹🚹🚹🚹🚹🚹🚹 |
| 5 | New York | United States | 🚹🚹🚹🚹🚹🚹🚹🚹 |
| 6 | Osaka-Kobe-Kyoto | Japan | 🚹🚹🚹🚹🚹🚹🚹 |
| 7 | Bombay | India | 🚹🚹🚹🚹🚹🚹🚹 |
| 8 | Calcutta | India | 🚹🚹🚹🚹🚹🚹🚹 |
| 9 | Rio de Janeiro | Brazil | 🚹🚹🚹🚹🚹🚹🚹 |
| 10 | Buenos Aires | Argentina | 🚹🚹🚹🚹🚹🚹 |

*Source:* Data from *Statistical Abstract of the United States,* 1994.

Key:  = 1 million people

 = ⊮2 million people

Use the pictograph to answer the questions.

1. What is the purpose of this pictograph?

2. How many people does each whole picture stand for?

3. How many people does each half picture stand for?

4. What is the population of each city?

• Tokyo-Yokohama?

• Seoul?

• New York?

• Bombay?

• Rio de Janeiro?

5. What countries have more than one city in the top ten?

6. How many more people live in Tokyo-Yokohama than in New York?

# Pie or Circle Graph

A **pie** or **circle graph** is used to show the relationship between the parts of something and the whole thing. The pie or circle represents the whole or 100%. Lines are used to create parts. The parts must add up to the whole or 100%.

U.S. Merchandise Exports by Regions in 1993

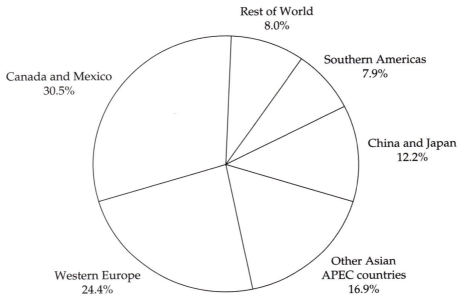

*Note:* The southern Americas include Central America, the Caribbean except for Cuba, and South America. Percentages do not add to 100 because of rounding.
*Source:* U.S. government.

Use the pie graph to answer the questions.

1. What is the purpose of this pie graph?

2. According to the graph, where did most exports go?

3. What percentage of U.S. exports went to Canada and Mexico?

4. Did more exports go to China and Japan or to Western Europe?

5. Do the percentages in the pie graph add to 100%? Why?

6. What is the source of this information?

A **bar graph** uses bars to show data. In the following bar graphs, the bars are vertical. At the top of each graph there is a title. Going up the left side, are numbers increasing from 0 to 25 to represent 1993 dollars. On the bottom are labels describing different levels of education. The height of each bar shows a 1993 dollar amount.

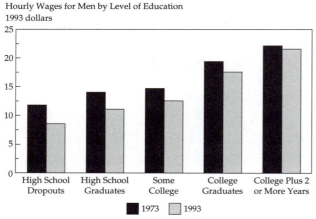

Hourly Wages for Men by Level of Education
1993 dollars

*Source:* U.S. government.

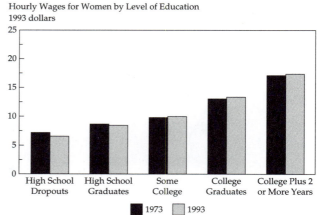

Hourly Wages for Women by Level of Education
1993 dollars

*Source:* U.S. government.

Use the bar graphs to answer the questions.

1. What is the purpose of each graph?

2. Have hourly wages for men with some college education increased or decreased since 1973? For women with some college education?

3. Which group had the highest hourly wages in 1973? In 1993?

4. Who had a higher hourly wage over the period 1973 to 1993, men or women?

5. Whose hourly wage has remained about the same over the 20 years, men or women?

In the following bar graph, the bars are horizontal. At the top of the graph there is a title. On the left side are categories of sports activities. Along the bottom are percentages from 0 to 45. The length of each bar shows the percentage of the U.S. population seven years old and older who participated in each of the activities during 1993.

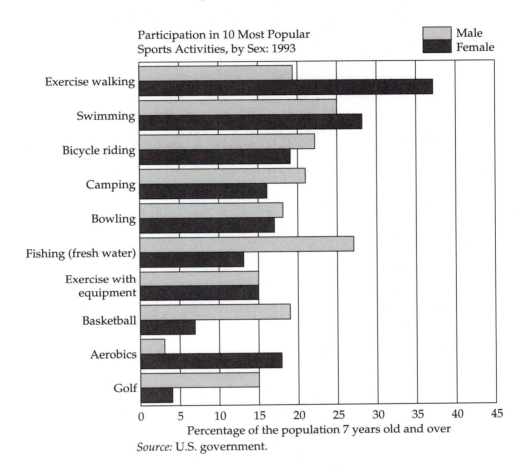

Participation in 10 Most Popular Sports Activities, by Sex: 1993

Percentage of the population 7 years old and over

*Source:* U.S. government.

Use the bar graph to answer the questions.

1. What is the purpose of this graph?

2. What was the most popular activity for males?

3. For females?

4. Did a higher percentage of males participate in camping or in basketball?

5. Did a higher percentage of women participate in bicycle riding or in exercising with equipment?

6. In which activities did a higher percentage of males than females participate?

7. In which activity did an equal percentage of males and females participate?

A **line graph** is used to show trends over a period of time. Read the title of the graph shown to learn what it is about. Then look to learn what information is presented on the left side and along the bottom. The lines on the graph show trends in federal government outlays (spending) and receipts (income). The difference between outlays and receipts represents the federal deficit (more spending than income).

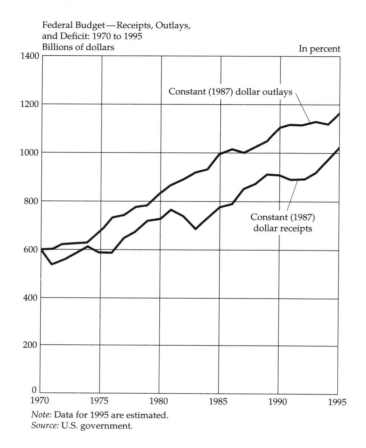

Federal Budget—Receipts, Outlays, and Deficit: 1970 to 1995

*Note:* Data for 1995 are estimated.
*Source:* U.S. government.

Use the line graph to answer the following questions.

1. What three types of information are shown in the line graph?

2. What has been the trend in federal government spending?

3. What has been the trend in federal government income?

4. What has happened to the federal deficit since 1970?

5. What happened to federal income in approximately 1983–1984?

6. What was the approximate size of the deficit in 1995?

*Diagram* **6-13**

A **diagram** is a drawing of something and its parts. The parts are sometimes labeled on the diagram. Other times the parts are identified in a key that accompanies the diagram.

**Structure of the Human Brain**

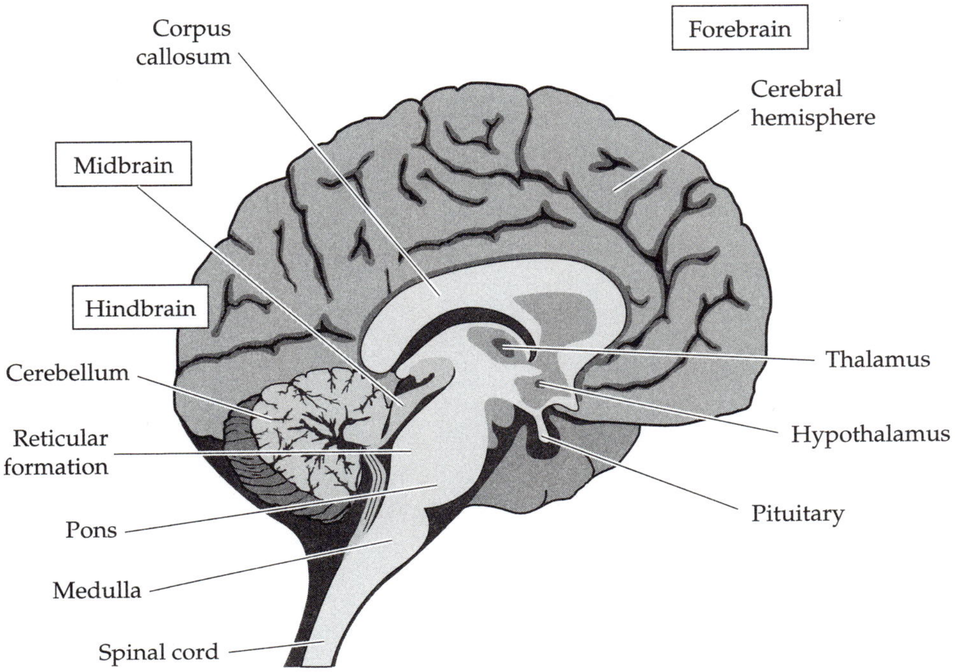

Use the diagram to answer the following questions:

1. What is the title of this diagram?


2. What can you learn from this diagram?


3. What are the three major structures of the brain?


4. Which of these structures would you find in the back of your head?


5. Front of your head?


6. Middle of your head?

Table 6-14

A **table** is used to show facts that would be difficult to understand if they were presented in written form. A table has a title that explains its purpose. Each column has a heading that tells what facts you will find in that column.

**Percentage of Americans Who Vote for President**

|  | 1980 | 1984 | 1988 | 1992 |
|---|---|---|---|---|
| *Overall* Americans Who Vote | 59% | 60% | 57% | 61% |
| *Age* |  |  |  |  |
| 18–20 | 36 | 37 | 33 | 39 |
| 21–24 | 43 | 44 | 38 | 46 |
| 25–34 | 55 | 55 | 48 | 53 |
| 35–44 | 64 | 64 | 61 | 64 |
| 45–64 | 69 | 70 | 68 | 70 |
| 65 and up | 65 | 68 | 69 | 70 |
| *Sex* |  |  |  |  |
| Male | 59 | 59 | 56 | 60 |
| Female | 59 | 61 | 58 | 62 |
| *Education* |  |  |  |  |
| Grade school only | 43 | 43 | 37 | 35 |
| High school dropout | 46 | 44 | 41 | 41 |
| High school graduate | 59 | 59 | 55 | 58 |
| College dropout | 67 | 68 | 65 | 69 |
| College graduate | 80 | 79 | 78 | 81 |

*Sources:* U.S. government.

Use the table above to answer the following questions:

1. What is the purpose of this table?

2. How many presidential elections are represented?

3. What conclusion can be drawn from the data for age?

4. What conclusion can be drawn from the data for sex?

5. What conclusion can be drawn from the data for education?

6. What two conclusions can be drawn from the overall data?

# Organizational Chart

An **organizational chart** shows how something is organized. Each box is labeled to show what it represents. Lines are used to show how the boxes are related. The boxes and lines together show the organization.

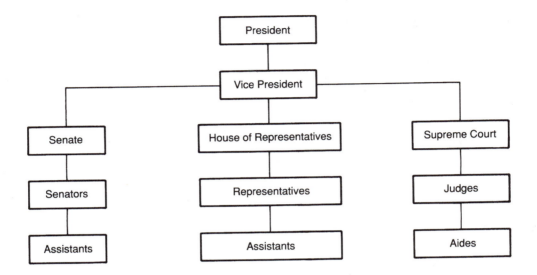

Use the organizational chart to answer the following questions:

1. What does this chart show?

2. What are the names of the three branches of the U.S. government?

3. Who is the highest ranking official?

4. What are the titles of people who work in the Senate?

5. Who is second in command?

6. Where do aides work?

7. For whom do they work?

A **flow chart** shows a process by which something works or occurs. Boxes, circles, or other shapes are used to show the parts of the process. Arrows are used to show the direction or order.

Stages of Mourning

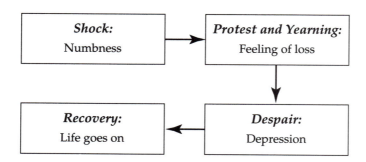

Use the organizational chart to answer the questions.

1. What does this flow chart show?

2. How many stages are shown?

3. What are the names of the stages? Write them in order.

4. In which stage does a person recognize his or her loss?

5. In which stage does one go on with one's life?

6. Do most people who lose a loved one go through all the stages of mourning shown?

See what you have learned about the use of visual aids.

1. What information do you find on these maps?

   Political

   Physical

   Road

   Weather

   Data

2. Complete the following statements:

   A pictograph is a graph in which

   A pie or circle graph is used to

   A bar graph uses

   A line graph is used to

3. When should each of the following be used?

   Diagram

   Table

   Organizational chart

   Flow chart

**6-1** 1. 7. 2. Guatemala, Belize, Honduras, El Salvador, Nicaragua, Costa Rica, Panama. 3. Guatemala, Belize. 4. Panama. 5. San Jose. 6. Honduras. 7. Rivas.

**6-2** 1. 10. 2. Alberta, British Columbia, Manitoba, New Brunswick, Newfoundland, Nova Scotia, Ontario, Prince Edward Island, Quebec, Saskatchewan. 3. 2. 4. Northwest Territories, Yukon Territory. 5. Yukon Territory. 6. Whitehorse. 7. Québec. 8. Ontario.

**6-3** 1. Andes. 2. Guiana Highlands, Brazilian Highlands. 3. Plateau of Bolivia. 4. Rivers. 5. Lake Titicaca. 6. Mountains and Highlands.

**6-4** 1. 87, 89, 91, 93. 2. Montpelier, Burlington. 3. 93. 4. 4. 5. 91. 6. Highway 91 and Road 2. 7. No.

**6-5** 1.

| Rain | Sunny | Low Pressure | Warm Front |
|------|-------|--------------|------------|
| ▨ | ☀ | L | ●●● |

2. Flurries. 3. Fargo, Minneapolis. 4. Phoenix, Miami. 5. Rain with temperature in the 70s. 6. H near Oklahoma City; L near Denver. 7. Southern Florida will get colder, Atlanta and Raleigh will get warmer, Boise and Billings will remain the same.

**6-6** 1. West to east. 2. Damp, then drying out. 3. Southeast. 4. Midwest and northeast. 5. Warmer weather. 6. Warm and cloudy.

**6-7** 1. Southwest Mountain. 2. Nevada, Utah, Colorado, Arizona, New Mexico. 3. Middle Atlantic. 4. 109%. 5. East North Central, South Atlantic, Pacific.

**6-8** 1. Show the population of the 10 largest cities in the world. 2. 2 million. 3. 1 million. 4. Tokyo–Yokohama 28 million, Seoul 19 million, New York 15 million, Bombay 14 million, Rio de Janeiro 13 million. 5. Japan, Brazil, India. 6. 13 million.

**6-9** 1. To show where U.S. exports went in 1993. 2. Canada and Mexico. 3. 30.5%. 4. Western Europe. 5. No. Percentages were rounded. 6. U.S. government.

**6-10** 1. Compare 1973 and 1993 hourly wages for men/women according to level of education. 2. Decreased for men; increased for women. 3. 1973, men with two or more years of college; 1993, same. 4. Men. 5. Women.

**6-11** 1. To show participation in the 10 most popular sports activities for ages 7 and older, by sex, during 1993. 2. Fishing. 3. Exercise walking. 4. Camping. 5. Bicycle riding. 6. Bicycle riding, camping, bowling, fishing, basketball, golf. 7. Exercising with equipment.

**6-12** 1. Federal government receipts, outlays, deficits. 2. Increased. 3. Increased. 4. Increased. 5. Decreased. 6. Approximately $175 billion.

**6-13** 1. Structure of the human brain. 2. The individual structures/parts that make up the human brain. 3. Forebrain, midbrain, hindbrain. 4. Hindbrain. 5. Forebrain. 6. Midbrain.

**6-14** Show percentage of Americans who voted for president in 1980, 1984, 1988, 1992. 2. 4. 3. As people get older a higher percentage vote. 4. A slightly higher percentage of females vote. 5. As people obtain more education, a higher percentage vote. 6. The percentage of voters has remained fairly constant. A large percentage of Americans do not vote.

**6-15** 1. Organization of U.S. Government. 2. Senate, House of Representatives, Supreme Court. 3. President. 4. Senators and Assistants. 5. Vice President. 6. Supreme Court. 7. Judges.

**6-16** 1. Stages of mourning. 2. 4. 3. Shock, protest and yearning, despair, recovery. 4. Protest and yearning. 5. Recovery. 6. Yes.

**6-17** 1. Political maps show boundaries, subdivisions, cities, and towns.
Physical maps show the features of the earth's surface.
Road maps show major highways and secondary roads.
Weather maps provide information on weather conditions.
Data maps show various kinds of information and data.

2. A pictograph is a graph in which pictures are used to provide information.
A pie or circle graph is used to show the relationship between the parts of something and the whole.
A bar graph uses bars to show data.
A line graph is used to show trends over a period of time.

3. A diagram should be used when you want to show something and its parts.
A table should be used when information is difficult to understand in written form.
An organizational chart should be used when you want to show how something is organized.
A flow chart should be used when you want to show the process by which something works or occurs.

## CHAPTER SEVEN

# Writing a Research Paper

## CHAPTER OBJECTIVES

1. Teach students a strategy for writing a research paper.
2. Teach students how to identify, locate, and document information needed to write a research paper.

## TITLES OF REPRODUCIBLE ACTIVITIES

7-1 Preparing a Research Paper
7-2 Choosing a Topic
7-3 Identifying Suitable Topics
7-4 Informative and Persuasive Topics
7-5 Practice Writing Persuasive Topics
7-6 Knowing If You Have Chosen a Good Topic
7-7 Focusing Your Research
7-8 Locating Sources of Information
7-9 Locating More Sources of Information
7-10 Preparing Bibliography Cards
7-11 Preparing More Bibliography Cards
7-12 Bibliography Cards for Electronic Sources of Information
7-13 Bibliography Cards for Internet References
7-14 Preparing Note Cards
7-15 Practice Making a Note Card
7-16 Writing an Outline for a Research Paper
7-17 Writing a Research Paper
7-18 Preparing Footnotes
7-19 Preparing a Bibliography
7-20 Preparing a Title Page
7-21 Preparing a Table of Contents
7-22 Final Checklist
7-23 Chapter Seven Mastery Assessment

## USING THE REPRODUCIBLE ACTIVITIES

After you have distributed a reproducible activity, here are suggestions for its use. Feel free to add further information, illustrations or examples. Wherever possible, relate the activity to actual subject area assignments.

### 7-1 Preparing a Research Paper

Use the activities in this chapter to take students through the steps of writing of a research paper. Students should develop their papers as they move through the activities.

Use 7-1 to explain the ten steps in writing a research paper. Have students use the space below each step to record notes.

### 7-2 Choosing a Topic

Use the introductory text to explain the difference between topics that are either too broad or too narrow and those that are suitable. Use the activity to provide students with practice identifying topic statements as too broad, too narrow, or suitable.

### 7-3 Identifying Suitable Topics

Review the difference between topics that are either too broad or too narrow and those that are suitable. Then have students rewrite the topics provided to make them suitable.

### 7-4 Informative and Persuasive Topics

Use the introductory text to explain the difference between informative papers that are meant to provide information to the reader and persuasive papers where the information provided is used to support a viewpoint. Have students complete the activity.

### 7-5 Practice Writing Persuasive Topics

Review the example provided and point out how the topic "Competition between Japanese and American automobile manufacturers "is informative, while the topic "Japanese cars are better than American cars" is persuasive. Use this exercise to give students practice rewriting informative topic statements into persuasive topic statements.

### 7-6  Knowing If You Have Chosen a Good Topic

Have students answer the four questions for the topic statements they wrote. Then have students choose one of their topic statements as the best one for their research papers. Have students explain why they chose that topic statement.

### 7-7  Focusing Your Research

Explain the importance of establishing parameters for research papers. Assist students to answer the questions for the topics they have chosen.

### 7-8  Locating Sources of Information

Review these sources of information previously covered in Chapters Four and Five. Use this activity to familiarize students with the process of gathering information from various sources. Students will have to go to the library to complete this activity. Encourage them to look for electronic sources of information such as CD ROM.

### 7-9  Locating More Sources of Information

Discuss the sources of information presented here. Have students go to the library to complete the activity. Delete the Internet portion if students do not have access to the Internet.

### 7-10  Preparing Bibliography Cards
### 7-11  Preparing More Bibliography Cards
### 7-12  Bibliography Cards for Electronic Sources of Information

### 7-13  Bibliography Cards for Internet References

Explain the importance of using bibliography cards to document the sources of information you use in writing research papers. Tell students they must prepare a separate bibliography card for each source of information. Use the samples to explain how bibliography cards are prepared for the most common sources. Describe the information found on each card and how the information is presented. Have students prepare bibliography cards for the eight types of sources of information in 7-10 through 7-13.

After students have completed 7-10 through 7-13, have them locate additional sources of information they need to write their papers. Direct students to prepare bibliography cards for these additional sources and for the sources they identified in 7-8 and 7-9.

### 7-14  Preparing Note Cards

Explain to students why they need to prepare note cards. Use the introductory text to guide students through alphabetizing and numbering all their bibliography cards. Point out that articles such as *the, a,* and *an* should not be considered the first word when alphabetizing.

Then explain how note cards are prepared and numbered. Emphasize that students should write notes in their own words. All quotations should be in the author's exact words and included within quotation marks. Page numbers should follow every quote. Emphasize the need for legible writing.

Review the sample bibliography card and its note card and have students answer the questions.

### 7-15  Practice Making a Note Card

Have students read the text from the book about the Great Lakes and create a note card. Then have students prepare note cards for all their bibliography cards.

### 7-16  Writing an Outline for a Research Paper

Use the introductory text and the sample outline to explain the format of an outline. Direct students to answer the questions. Then have students organize their notes from their note cards and write an outline for their papers.

### 7-17  Writing a Research Paper

Use the text to explain to students how to write the first draft of their papers. Help students understand the information that belongs in each section of the paper: introduction, body, and conclusion. Show students how to use the Revising Checklist to improve their rough draft and write their papers.

### 7-18  Preparing Footnotes

Use the introductory text to explain and demonstrate why and how footnotes are prepared. Have students answer the questions. Tell students how you want them to show footnotes in their research papers. Then have them add footnotes.

### 7-19 Preparing a Bibliography

Students need to know that a bibliography is an alphabetical list of all the sources of information they consulted to prepare their research papers. Use the introductory text to explain how a bibliography is prepared. Have students prepare a bibliography using the bibliography cards provided. Then have students prepare the bibliography for their papers using their bibliography cards.

### 7-20 Preparing a Title Page

Use the introductory text and sample title page to explain how to prepare a title page. Then have students prepare a title page for their research papers.

### 7-21 Preparing a Table of Contents

Use the introductory text and sample table of contents to explain how to prepare a table of contents. Have students use the information provided to prepare a table of contents. Then have them prepare a table of contents for their research papers.

### 7-22 Final Checklist

Discuss with the students how they can use the Final Checklist to be sure their research papers are in the correct form to hand in to teachers. Then have them answer the questions.

### 7-23 Chapter Seven Mastery Assessment;

Have students complete this assessment at any point you feel they have learned the ten steps in writing a research paper. Review the results of the assessment with the students. Provide additional instruction as necessary.

Here are the important steps to follow to write a research paper. As your teacher discusses each step, write down the important things you need to remember about each step.

**Step 1.** Choosing a topic

**Step 2.** Defining and locating sources of information

**Step 3.** Preparing bibliography cards

**Step 4.** Preparing note cards

**Step 5.** Preparing the outline for the paper

**Step 6.** Writing the paper

**Step 7.** Preparing footnotes

**Step 8.** Preparing the bibliography

**Step 9.** Preparing the title page and table of contents

**Step 10.** Final proofing

The first step in writing a research paper is to choose a **topic.** Your topic should not be too broad or too narrow. If your topic is too broad, you will not be able to complete the research paper in the number of pages assigned by your teacher. If your topic is too narrow, you will not find enough information. Be sure to select a topic in which you are interested.

Read each of the following topic statements. One is too broad, one is too narrow, and the other is suitable. Read to learn why.

The effects of pollution on the lives of people throughout the world.

This statement is too broad because it would take too long to obtain information on people who live in every country in the world.

The effects of pollution on mallard ducks.

This statement is too narrow because it limits the topic only to mallard ducks. Although there may be a lot of information available on pollution, there is probably very little on how pollution affects mallard ducks.

The effects of pollution on people who get their water from the Great Lakes.

Here is a topic that is suitable for a research paper. The topic is limited to water pollution and to the Great Lakes. There will be sufficient information on both pollution and the Great Lakes.

Read each of the following topic statements. For each, tell if the topic is too broad, too narrow, or suitable. Explain your answer.

**1.** Agriculture in America _____

_____

**2.** Raising soybeans in southwest Arkansas _____

_____

**3.** Soybean production in the United States _____

_____

**4.** National parks in the U.S. _____

_____

**5.** Mating habits of the great blue heron nesting by the Anhinga Trail in the Everglades National Park _____

_____

**6.** The preservation of our National Parks _____

_____

In 7-2, you learned that your topic should be neither too broad nor too narrow. Study the examples and then rewrite the topics that follow to make each one suitable.

**Too Broad:**    The automobile industry
**Too Narrow:**   Using robots to build cars in Tokyo, Japan
**Suitable:**     Competition between Japanese and American auto manufacturers

1. Drugs in America

2. Using computers to teach spelling of one-syllable words

3. The history of cartoons

4. World hunger

5. Ankle injuries in high school football

6. The origin of the word *spaghetti*

All research papers provide information, but sometimes the information is used to support a point of view or to argue against an alternative point of view. Read the following topics and write **I** next to informative topics and **P** next to persuasive topics.

1. _____ Homeless children in America

2. _____ Movies should not be rated

3. _____ Some athletes with AIDS should be banned from playing

4. _____ The message of rap music

5. _____ Public high schools should not have a dress code

6. _____ The war in Bosnia

7. _____ Athletes and AIDS

8. _____ The need for increased funding for the homeless

9. _____ Movie themes of the 1990s

10. _____ American soldiers should not have been sent to Bosnia

11. _____ The need for drug testing in public schools

12. _____ Rap music causes teenage violence

13. _____ Drugs in our schools

14. _____ Ten ways to eat healthfully

In 7-4, you learned the difference between informative and persuasive topics. Study the examples and then rewrite each informative topic to make it persuasive.

**Informative:** Competition between Japanese and American automobile manufacturers
**Persuasive:** Japanese cars are better than American cars

1. Advertising on television

2. Dress codes in public schools

3. Political parties in the United States

4. Gun control in the United States

5. Day care centers for working mothers

6. The American government's foreign policy

7. Capital punishment in the United States

8. Salaries for professional athletes

Here are some important questions you should answer about any topic you choose. These questions will help you know if the topic you have chosen is a good one.

Write at least two topics about which you would like to write a research paper.

1. _____

2. _____

3. _____

Now answer these questions for the first topic you wrote.

- Is the topic too broad, too narrow, or suitable?

Remember, if the topic is too broad or too narrow you will find it difficult to complete the paper within the number of pages assigned by your teacher.

- Is there enough factual information available to you on the topic?

Check in the library to see if there are enough references available to get the factual information you need on the topic. Make sure you have at least as many references as required by your teacher.

- Are you interested in this topic?

Be sure to select a topic in which you are interested. It takes a lot of time to do the research and writing. If you are not interested in the topic, you will probably not do a very good job of writing the paper.

- Will your teacher approve the topic?

Show your written topic statement to your teacher and ask for approval. Do not begin to work on a topic unless your teacher has approved it. Your teacher will probably have a book in which all the research topics are recorded by students in the class. Usually teachers will not allow more than one student to work on the same topic.

On which one of your topics would you like to write a research paper?

_____

_____

Why did you choose this one?

_____

_____

Write the topic for your paper.

Before you begin to write your paper and search for information, you must be specific about the kind of paper you will write and the information you will need. Answering these questions will help you focus your research. Use a check (✔) to show your answers.

1. Will this be a paper only, or is there an oral presentation as well?

   Written paper _____ Paper and oral presentation/speech _____

2. Which visual aids do you need to include?

   Pictures _____ Photographs _____ Graphs _____ Charts _____ Maps _____

   List any other visual aids you will need.

3. What should be the length of your paper?

   1 to 5 pages _____ 6 to 10 pages _____ More than 10 pages _____

4. Is your paper informative _____ or persuasive _____?

5. Do you need any historical information? Yes _____ No _____

6. Do you need information from within the last year? Yes _____ No _____

7. Are there terms or concepts associated with this topic that you do not understand?

   Yes _____ No _____ List them.

8. Are there questions that must be answered with numbers or statistics?

   Yes _____ No _____ If yes, write them here.

# Locating Sources of Information

Write the topic you used for 7-7.

Find information on your topic in each of the following sources. For each source, write its title and call number. Check (✔) whether it is in print or electronic format. Try to include at least one source that is in electronic format.

**Encyclopedias**

Title:                                                Call Number:

Print _____ Electronic _____

**Other Reference Books**

Title:                                                Call Number:

Print _____ Electronic _____

**Magazines**

Title:                                                Call Number:

Print _____ Electronic _____

**Newspapers**

Title:                                                Call Number:

Print _____ Electronic _____

**Scholarly Journals**

Title:                                                Call Number:

Print _____ Electronic _____

**Books**

Title:                                                Call Number:

Print _____ Electronic _____

Write the topic you used for 7-8.

Find information on your topic in each of the following three sources. For each, write its title and check (✔) the format in which it was found.

**Audio/visual.**    Sources of information that require you to watch or to listen.

Title:

TV _____    Radio _____    Video _____    Film _____    Audiocassette _____

**Primary sources.**    Persons who have first-hand experience with an event or a topic are primary sources of information. Information from primary sources might be in the form of interviews, diaries, journals, oral histories, or newspaper accounts. Primary sources provide an interesting "I was there" perspective.

Title:

Print _____    Electronic _____    Microform _____

**Internet.**    The Internet can be used to find information. The World Wide Web (WWW) is a particularly good tool to locate information on the Internet. Many communities also have a FreeNet for their residents. Some school libraries and many public libraries provide access to the WWW and/or the local FreeNet for library users.

Title of information found:

World Wide Web (WWW) _____    Gopher _____    FreeNet _____

Bibliography cards document sources of information used when writing research papers. Examine the sample bibliography cards prepared for four basic sources of information.

```
Reference Book
"Water Pollution."
New Times Encyclopedia
12th ed. 1996
```

```
Magazine Article
Rockman, Julie. "Examining
the Shores of the Great Lakes."
Preserving Mother Nature
Oct. 1996: 3-6.
```

```
Book
Hanson, Tom. Water Pollution.
Great Falls, Iowa: Appleton Press, 1996.
```

```
Newspaper Article
"Pollutants Destroying the Great Lakes."
Detroit Gazette 14 Oct. 1995: 5.
```

Refer to the sample cards to help you prepare bibliography cards for each source of information.

**Reference Book** article entitled, "Polluting America's Great Lakes." Found on pages 45–46 of the 14th edition of the *World Encyclopedia,* 1995.

**Magazine Article** entitled, "Stop Polluting My Drinking Water." Francis Duda is the author. The article appeared in the *Great Lakes Monthly Magazine* on page 44 of the September 25, 1995, issue.

**Book** entitled *Water All Around Us.* Jake Brown is the author. University of Michigan Press, Lansing, Michigan, is the publisher. Published in 1996.

**Newspaper Article** entitled "What I saw on the Beach Made Me Sick" found on page B24 of the *Minneapolis Times* on October 1, 1995.

Examine the sample bibliography cards prepared for audio/visual and primary sources of information.

```
Audio/Visual Source
Cruising the Waters of Lake Michigan.
Videocassette. 1996. 60 mn., VHS
STAR Educational Services, 1996.
```

```
Primary Source
Billips, Jason. Water Supervisor,
Marquette, Michigan 49780
Personal conversation, 20 Oct. 1995.
```

Refer to the sample cards to help you prepare bibliography cards for each source of information.

Audiocassette tape made in 1996, entitled *Boating the Great Lakes,* that is 30 minutes long and distributed by LTM Audiotapes, Milwaukee, Wisconsin.

Conversation with Kathy Clark, Director of Public Works, Chicago, Illinois, on September 16, 1995.

# Bibliography Cards for Electronic Sources of Information

**7-12**

Examine the sample bibliography card for an electronic source of information. Headings are provided for each part of the citation shown on the card.

```
Author                 Crawley, James W.
Title of Article       "Women on Warships: Navy Determined to
                       Prove Gender is No Sea-Going Issue."
Title of Publication   The San Diego Union Tribune
Date of Article        31 May 1995: A1.
Title of Database      CD NewsBank Comprehensive
Publication Medium     CD ROM
Name of Vendor         NewsBank
Date of CD ROM         1 Dec. 1994-6 Jan. 1996
```

The example provided is for an article from a newspaper on CD ROM. You may also find articles from magazines, journals, and encyclopedias on CD ROM. They may be full text or citation only. Although the publication medium in the example is CD ROM, you may find articles in other electronic formats. Refer to the sample card to help you prepare a bibliography card for the electronic source of information that follows.

Magazine article entitled, "Criminal Records: Gangsta Rap and the Culture of Violence." John Leland is the author. The article appeared in Newsweek on pages 60–64, in the November 29, 1993, issue. The 1995 disc for SIRS (Social Issues Resources Series) on CD ROM was used. SIRS is also the name of the company.

**Author:**

**Title of Article:**

**Title of Publication:**

**Date of Article:**

**Title of Database:**

**Publication Medium:**

**Name of Vendor:**

**Date of CD ROM:**

Copyright © 1997 by Allyn and Bacon

Examine the sample bibliography card for information found on the Internet.

```
Author                United States. National Park Service.
Title                 How National Park Units Are Established.
Date of Information   13 Apr. 1995.
Site                  National Park Service.
Address (URL)         http://www.nps.gov/pub_aff/issues/
Online Service        howpark_.html
Online Service        World Wide Web, Netscape.
Date Accessed         29 Feb. 1996.
```

Refer to the sample card to prepare a bibliography card for the following information found on the Internet.

There is a World Wide Web site called "A Working Hip-Hop Chronology" that can be found at:

http://www.ai.mit.edu/~isbell/HFh/hiphop/rap_history.html

The information was written by Russell A. Potter, Ph.D. (a.k.a. Professa RAP). There is no date given for when this information was written, but it was found online on February 29, 1996, using Netscape to search the WWW (World Wide Web).

**Author (if known):**

**Title:**

**Date of Information:**

**Site:**

**Address: (URL)**

**Online Service**

**Date Accessed:**

Use note cards to record notes from each source you use when writing a research paper. Before you prepare note cards, you must first arrange your bibliography cards in alphabetical order by the first word on the card. Then number all the cards starting with 1 for the first card. The number should be written in the upper right-hand corner of the bibliography card. Now you are ready to prepare note cards.

When preparing note cards, use two numbers separated by a dash. For example, in a note card numbered 4-1, 4 shows that the notes are for the source listed on bibliography card 4, and 1 shows this is the first card used to record notes from this source. If you need more than one note card to record notes from this source, the second card would be numbered 4-2, and so on for as many note cards as you need. The number of the note card should be written in the upper right-hand corner of the card. Circle the number to keep it separate from other numbers you might write when taking notes.

Write notes in your own words whenever possible. Place quotation marks around all quotes. Write the page number on which each quote appears. Look at the following bibliography card and a note card that goes with it.

Bibliography Card

```
Baxson, Bill.   Can't Drink the Water or Eat the Fish.      4
                South Bend, Indiana: Dwag Press, 1996.
```

Note Card

```
"The water contains mercury and other chemicals." p. 23    (4-2)
Many fish are dying.
Fishing industry is hurting.
People are worried about their jobs.
New, tough laws are making things better.
The lakes will be safe again and soon.
```

1. What do you use to place your bibliography cards in alphabetical order?

2. Where do you write the number of a bibliography card?

3. Can a bibliography card have more than one note card?

4. When should you use quotation marks on a note card?

5. Why is the number 4-2 circled on the note card?

6. What does 4 tell you?

7. What does the -2 tell you?

# Practice Making a Note Card

Complete the first note card that goes with this bibliography card.

**BIBLIOGRAPHY CARD**

```
Zayre, Terry.
"The Great Lakes are Healing."
Science Today July 1996: 56-59.
```

Here is information from this source.

Everyone has heard of the Great Lakes. They border a number of states in the United States and a number of provinces in Canada. They are the largest source of fresh water in the world.

Things are getting better in the Great Lakes since many industries have stopped discharging polluted water directly into the lakes. The water is safe to drink and the fish are once again safe to eat. It took 10 years to turn things around but it has finally happened.

It took cooperation between government and industry to solve the program. Now everyone has to be responsible for keeping the lakes clean and healthy. The Great Lakes are an important source of water, food, and recreation for many Americans and Canadians.

**NOTE CARD**

To write an outline for a research paper, begin by organizing notes from the note cards into main topics, subtopics, details, and subdetails. Then write the title of the paper near the top of a blank piece of paper. As shown in the sample outline below, write the Roman numeral I and after it the first main topic. Use capital letters before each subtopic that goes with the main topic. Use Arabic numerals before each detail that goes with the subtopic. Use small letters before each subdetail. Repeat this for each main topic until you have completed the outline. You can write the main topics, subtopics, details, and subdetails as sentences, phrases, or single words.

   Examine this sample outline and answer the questions.

*The Effects of Pollution on People Who Get Their Water from the Great Lakes*

   I. Water for drinking
      A. Mercury
      B. Iron ore
      C. Paper industries
         1. Getting the wood to the paper mills
            a. truck
            b. railroad
            c. floating logs down rivers
         2. Chemicals used to make paper
      D. Tourists add to the problem
  II. Fish for eating
      A. Chemical contamination
      B. Fewer fish
      C. Takes years to reproduce
 III. Recreation
      A. There will be less fun in the sun if something isn't done soon.
      B. Recreational boaters cause some of the problem.
      C. People are scared to swim in the water.

**1.** How should you begin preparing an outline for a research paper?

**2.** What is the title for this paper?

**3.** How many subtopics are found for the main topic "Fish for eating"?

**4.** Write the two details that go with the subtopic "Paper industries."

**5.** Write the three subdetails that go with this subtopic.

**6.** List the main topics.

Begin by writing a rough draft of your research paper. Start by writing the title at the top of the page. Then write an introduction that tells the reader what the paper will be about. Use your outline and note cards to write the body of the paper. As you write, insert headings and visual aids that will help the reader understand your topic. When you have finished writing about your topic, write a conclusion. The conclusion tells the reader what you have learned about the topic or summarizes your point of view. Leave at least one-inch margins on all sides and double space the draft to leave room for revising. Number each page in the top right-hand corner as you write.

## Revising Checklist

When you have finished writing a rough draft, reread it carefully and answer the questions. If you answer NO to any of the questions, revise your draft until you can answer YES to all questions.

1. Does the introduction clearly introduce the topic?

2. Did I include headings to help the reader understand the topic?

3. Does the body of the paper contain all facts needed?

4. Does each paragraph contain a main idea?

5. Does every paragraph add something to the paper?

6. Did I choose the best words to explain ideas?

7. Does my conclusion follow from the facts?

8. Did I spell all words correctly?

9. Did I capitalize words as needed?

10. Is there subject–verb agreement in all cases?

11. Are tenses consistent?

12. Are all sentences complete?

13. Did I use quotation marks to identify all quotations?

14. Have I reread the paper several times to find ways to improve it?

15. Did I number the pages correctly?

Credit must be given to sources from which you take quotations or major ideas. In a research paper, credit is given by using **footnotes.** On the page, a footnote reference number is written after the material for which credit is being given. The number is slightly raised above the line. Most often the footnotes are placed at the bottom of the page on which the quotation or main idea appears. A line is drawn to separate the text from the footnotes. Here is an example of a footnoted page. Notice how numbers are used in the text and in the footnotes to show how the references go together.

The most common shoe size for men is size nine and for women it is size seven.[1] According to Donald Blake in the *Shoe Manufacturer's Journal,* "men and women are growing bigger feet."[2]

1. Phil Harris, Shoe Sales (New York: York Press, 1996) 34.
2. Donald Blake, "Feet Are Getting Bigger," Shoe Manufacturers' Journal, Vol. 11, September 1996, p. 56.

Sometimes teachers prefer to have all the footnotes on one page at the end of the paper. When footnotes are listed at the end of a paper, the same format is used for writing the footnotes. The footnotes are numbered in the order the information is presented in the paper. Ask your teacher which way footnotes should be shown in your research paper.

**1.** When should you use footnotes?

**2.** In what two places can footnotes appear?

**3.** Who decides where the footnotes should appear in a research paper?

**4.** Is the same format used to write footnotes no matter where they appear?

**5.** What separates your writing from the footnotes when they are at the bottom of a page?

At the end of a research paper you must provide a list of all the sources you used to gather information for the paper. This list of sources is called the **bibliography.** Here is a sample bibliography.

## Bibliography

Abbott, James. Director of the Regional Pollution Center, Zephyrhills, Florida 33541. Personal letter, 12 Nov. 1996.

"Covering Up the Pollution Story." <u>Atlanta Daily News</u> 9 Dec 1995: 4.

Frank, Steven. "What Are They Doing to Our Water?" <u>Today's Health</u>, Jan. 1995: 62–67.

"Pollution." <u>World Encyclopedia</u>. 1995.

*Ruining Our World through Neglect.* Videocassette. Save Our Planet, 1993.

Thompson, Robert. <u>Our Polluted World: What Will We Leave for Our Children</u>? Chicago: Delta Press, 1996.

Thurston, Harry. "The Fatal Shore: The Mystery of Marine Mammal Strandings." <u>Canadian Geographic</u>. Jan./Feb. 1995: 60–68. SIRS. CD ROM. Winter 1995.

United States. Environmental Protection Agency. <u>The Quality of Our Nation's Water</u>. Environmental Protection Agency. http://www.epa.gov/305b/sum1.html World Wide Web, Netscape. 5 Mar. 1996.

To prepare a bibliography, you need a blank sheet of paper and your bibliography cards. Write the word "Bibliography" in the center of a line two inches below the top of the sheet of paper. Then check to be sure all your bibliography cards are in alphabetical order by the first word on each card. Now write the information as it appears on each bibliography card. Indent the second and following lines as shown on the sample bibliography above.

On a blank sheet of paper, prepare a bibliography using the sample bibliography cards that follow.

Zayre, Albert. The Russian State.
N.Y.: Williams House Publishers, 1996.

Mann, Mark. "The Mongols Take Over Russia."
Historical Review Apr. 1996:10-12.

Bos, Candy. Director of the Miami Historical
    Center,
Miami, Florida 33122.
Personal letter, 25 May 1995.

"Russian Tsars." Encyclopedia of Nations.
N.Y.: College Press, 1995.

"Government in the Early Years of the USSR."
San Francisco Daily News 15 June 1996:20.

Touring the Kremlin.
Videocassette. International Video Productions,
1986.

Thompson, Mary Ellen. Russian language teacher,
Willow School, Minneapolis, Minnesota 48767.
Personal conversation, 4 June 1995.

Striker, Sally. "Beautiful Icons."
Modern Art  July 1996:23-27.

Corwin, Julie and Stanglin, Douglas.
"The Looting of Russia."
US News and World Report.  7 Mar. 1994:36.
SIRS CD ROM SIRS, Winter 1995.

Beard, Robert. Russian History.
Bucknell University, Russian Program
http://www.bucknell.edu/departments
    /russian/history.html
World Wide Web, Netscape.
5 Mar. 1996.

The **title page** is the first page of the research paper. It includes the title of the research paper, the name of the writer, and the date on which the paper is due. Look at the sample title page as you read the information in the box about it.

> To prepare the title page, you need a blank piece of paper. Three inches from the top of the sheet of paper, write or type the title using all capital letters. Be sure to center the title. About six inches from the top and bottom of the sheet of paper and centered, type the word "by." Two lines below the word "by," and centered, write your name. Two lines below your name, and centered, write the date the paper is due.

SOYBEAN PRODUCTION IN THE UNITED STATES

by

Mary Hardy

January 17, 1997

What information is included on the title page?

The **table of contents** is the second page of the research paper. Look at the sample table of contents as you read the information in the box about it.

To prepare the table of contents, you need a blank piece of paper. Three inches from the top of the sheet of paper and centered, write or type the words "Table of Contents." Capitalize only the first letter of the word "Table" and the first letter of "Contents." Leave a one-inch margin on both the left and right sides of the piece of paper. The table of contents lists the main topics and important subtopics, and the pages on which each is introduced in a research paper. Capitalize each major word in each entry in the table of contents.

## Table of Contents

|  | Page |
|---|---|
| Introduction | 1 |
| Northeastern states | 2 |
| Midwestern states | 3 |
| Southern states | 5 |
| Western states | 9 |
| Conclusion | 10 |
| Bibliography | 12 |

Use the following information to prepare a Table of Contents.
Lumbering in the forests of California. By Jane Diane Ross. Paper due January 21, 1997.

Introduction, page 1
A land of many trees, page 2
Rapid growth in population, page 6

More housing needed, page 8
Saving the forest, page 12
Conclusion, page 15
Bibliography, page 17

When you have finished writing your research paper, reread it carefully and answer the questions. If you answer YES to all questions, your paper is ready to be handed in to your teacher. If you answer NO to any of the questions, revise your paper until you can answer YES to all questions. Then your paper is ready to be handed in.

### Final Checklist

1. Do I have a title page?

2. Do I have a table of contents?

3. Are the pages numbered correctly?

4. Have I included all the footnotes?

5. Do I have a bibliography?

6. Do I have a second copy for my files?

7. Do I have a folder in which to place the original copy to hand in to my teacher?

See what you have learned about writing a research paper.

1. How many important steps must you follow to write a research paper?

2. What problem will you have if you choose a topic that is too broad? Too narrow?

3. Explain the difference between an informative and a persuasive research paper.

4. List at least five different kinds of sources that you may use to locate information for your topic.

5. On a note card, what does "6-2" mean?

6. Label each part of the following outline:

   I. _____

      A. _____

         1. _____

            a. _____

7. What is the first version of a research paper called?

8. Why must you use footnotes?

9. What is a bibliography?

10. What is the first page of the research paper called?

    The second page?

11. What is the purpose of the Final Checklist?

**7-1** Notes will vary

**7-2** 1. Too broad. There are many forms of agriculture in America. 2. Too narrow. Too small a geographical area on which to focus. 3. Suitable. Refers to a specific crop in a large enough geographical area. 4. Too broad. There are too many national parks and too many topics related to them. 5. Too narrow. Focuses on a specific topic for a specific bird in a specific location in one national park. 6. Suitable. Refers to one specific issue for all the national parks.

**7-3** Answers will vary

**7-4** 1. I. 2. P. 3. P. 4. I. 5. P. 6. I. 7. I. 8. P. 9. I. 10. P. 11. P. 12. P. 13. I. 14. I.

**7-5** Answers will vary.

**7-6** Answers will vary.

**7-7** Answers will vary.

**7-8** Answers will vary.

**7-9** Answers will vary.

**7-10** Reference Book    "Polluting America's Great Lakes." World Book Encyclopedia 14th ed. 1995

Magazine Article    Duda, Francis. "Stop Polluting My Drinking Water." Great Lakes Monthly Magazine 25 Sept. 1995: 45–46.

Book    Brown, Jake. Water All Around Us. Lansing, Michigan: University of Michigan Press, 1996.

Newspaper Article    "What I Saw on the Beach Made Me Sick." Minneapolis Times 1 Oct. 1996: B24.

**7-11** Audio/Visual    Boating the Great Lakes. Audiocassette. 1990. 30 minutes. LTM Audiotapes, 1996.

Primary    Clark, Kathy. Director of Public Works, Chicago, Illinois Personal conversation, 16 Sept. 1995.

**7-12** Electronic Source    Leland, John. "Criminal Records: Gangsta Rap and the Culture of Violence." Newsweek 29 Nov. 1993: 60–64. SIRS (Social Issues Resources Series) CD ROM SIRS, 1995

**7-13** Internet   Potter, Russell A.
A Working Hip-Hop Chronology.
No Date
A Working Hip-Hop Chronology
http://www.ai.mit.edu/~isbell/HFh/
hiphop/rap_history.html
World Wide Web, Netscape
29 Feb. 1996

**7-14** 1. First word on the card.
   2. Upper-right hand corner.
   3. Yes.
   4. When you use quotes.
   5. To separate it from other numbers you might write when taking notes.
   6. The notes are for the source listed on bibliography card 4.
   7. It is the second note card used to record notes from the source listed on bibliography card 4.

**7-15** Answers will vary.

**7-16** 1. Organize notes into main topics, subtopics, details, and subdetails.
   2. "The Effects of Pollution on People Who Get Their Water from the Great Lakes."
   3. Three.
   4. Getting the wood to the paper mills; Chemicals used to make paper.
   5. truck; railroad; floating logs down rivers.
   6. Water for drinking; fish for eating; recreation.

**7-17** Answers will vary.

**7-18** 1. When credit must be given to sources from which you take quotations or major ideas.
   2. At the bottom of a page or at the end of the paper.
   3. Your teacher.
   4. Yes.
   5. A line that is drawn to separate the footnotes from the text of the paper.

**7-19 BIBLIOGRAPHY**

Beard, Robert. Russian History. Bucknell University. Russian Program.   http://www.bucknell.edu/departments/russian/history.html World Wide Web, Netscape. 5 Mar. 1996.

Bos, Candy. Director of the Miami Historical Center, Miami, Florida 33122. Personal letter, 25 May 1990.

Corwin, Julie and Stanglin, Douglas. "The Looting of Russia." US News and World Report 7 Mar. 1994: 36. SIRS. CD ROM. SIRS, Winter 1995.

"Government in the Early Years of the USSR." San Francisco Daily News, 15 June 1996: 20.

Mann, Mark. "The Mongols Take Over Russia." Historical Review. Apr. 1990: 10–12.

"Russian Tzars." <u>Encyclopedia of Nations</u>. NY: College Press, 1995.

Striker, Sally. "Beautiful Icons." <u>Modern Art</u>. July 1996: 23–27.

Thompson, Mary Ellen, Russian Language Teacher, Willow School, Minneapolis, Minnesota 48767. Personal conversation, 4 June 1995.

<u>Touring the Kremlin</u>. Videocassette. International Video Productions, 1986.

Zayre, Albert. <u>The Russian State</u>. NY: Williams House, 1996.

**7-20** Title of the research paper; name of the writer; date on which the paper is due.

**7-21**

---

## Table of Contents

|  | Page |
|---|---|
| Introduction | 1 |
| A Land of Many Trees | 2 |
| Rapid Growth in Population | 6 |
| More Housing Needed | 8 |
| Saving the Forest | 12 |
| Conclusion | 15 |
| Bibliography | 17 |

---

**7-22** Answers will vary.

**7-23**
1. Ten.
2. Will not be able to complete the paper in the number of pages assigned; will not be able to find enough information.
3. Informative—provides information; persuasive—supports a point of view or argues against an alternative point of view.
4. Encyclopedias; other reference books; magazines; newspapers; scholarly journals; books; audiovisual; primary sources; Internet.
5. Bibliography card 6, note card 2.
6. I. Main Topic
      A. Subtopic
         1. Detail
            a. Subdetail
7. Rough draft.
8. To give credit to sources from which you take quotations or major ideas.
9. A list of all the sources used to gather information for a paper.
10. Title Page; Table of Contents.
11. To be sure a paper is ready to be handed in.

## CHAPTER EIGHT

# Preparing for and Taking Tests

## CHAPTER OBJECTIVES

1. Teach students a five-day strategy for preparing to take tests.
2. Teach students strategies for taking different types of tests.

## TITLES OF REPRODUCIBLE ACTIVITIES

8-1　Getting Ready for a Test
8-2　Five-Day Test Preparation Plan
8-3　Taking a Test
8-4　Learning about Multiple-Choice Tests
8-5　Guidelines for Taking Multiple-Choice Tests
8-6　More Guidelines for Taking Multiple-Choice Tests
8-7　Guidelines for Taking True/False Tests
8-8　Practice Taking a True/False Test
8-9　Guidelines for Taking Matching Tests
8-10　Guidelines for Taking Completion Tests
8-11　Using the QUOTE Strategy When Taking Essay Tests: Question
8-12　More Direction Words
8-13　Using QUOTE: Underline
8-14　Using QUOTE: Organize
8-15　Using Graphic Organizers
8-16　Writing an Answer for an Essay Test Item
8-17　Using QUOTE: Time
8-18　Using QUOTE: Evaluate
8-19　Chapter Eight Mastery Assessment

## USING THE REPRODUCIBLE ACTIVITIES

After you have distributed a reproducible activity, here are suggestions for its use. Feel free to add further information, illustrations, or examples. Wherever possible, relate the activity to actual subject area assignments.

### 8-1  Getting Ready for a Test

Discuss the importance of having a plan for preparing for a test. Have students read the three things they should do to get ready to take a test. Then have students write a summary paragraph explaining what to do to get ready for a test.

### 8-2  Five-Day Test Preparation Plan

Have students read the Five-Day Test Preparation Plan. Point out to students that on Day Three they will be using remembering strategies they previously learned. Then have students write a description of what they should do on each day. They can include any special things they would do.

### 8-3  Taking a Test

Have students read the five things to do to improve their test scores. Review the purpose of an acronym and the use of DETER to remember the five things to do. Then have students write what each letter in DETER reminds them to do.

### 8-4  Learning about Multiple-Choice Tests

Use the activity to familiarize students with two types of multiple-choice items. Provide additional examples from various subject area materials and/or tests. Then have students write test items using the information provided.

### 8-5  Guidelines for Taking Multiple-Choice Tests

Have students read the guidelines for answering multiple-choice test items. Answer any questions students have and then have them complete the multiple-choice test.

### 8-6 More Guidelines for Taking Multiple-Choice Tests

Have students read the additional guidelines for answering multiple-choice test items. Answer any questions students have, and then have them complete the multiple-choice test.

### 8-7 Guidelines for Taking True/False Tests

Have students read each guideline and answer the true/false question that follows.

### 8-8 Practice Taking a True/False Test

Have students complete the true/false test. For items 7, 8, and 9, have students write a reason for each answer.

### 8-9 Guidelines for Taking Matching Tests

Have students read the guidelines for doing well on a matching test. Then have students complete the matching test and answer the questions that follow.

### 8-10 Guidelines for Taking Completion Tests

Have students read the description of a completion test item and examine the sample items with the missing part in different places. Then have students read the guidelines for doing well on completion tests. Finally, have students write a summary that tells what they learned about taking a completion test.

### 8-11 Using the QUOTE Strategy When Taking Essay Tests: Question

Introduce students to the acronym QUOTE. Explain that QUOTE should be used to remember the five steps in a strategy for taking essay tests. Q reminds students to look for and bracket [   ] direction words in essay items. Be certain students understand the meaning of each of the three direction words. Have students complete the activity.

### 8-12 More Direction Words

Clarify any questions students have about the nine additional direction words introduced in this activity. Then have the students complete the activity.

### 8-13  Using QUOTE: Underline

<u>U</u> reminds students to underline key words to obtain a clear understanding of the essay item. Show how this is done using the sample essay item. Then have students bracket the direction word and underline key words in each essay item that follows.

### 8-14  Using QUOTE: Organize

<u>O</u> reminds students to organize the facts needed to answer an essay item. Review what students should do for this step. Help students locate the resources they need to complete the activity. Students will use their facts in Activity 8-16.

### 8-15  Using Graphic Organizers

Show students how the four graphic organizers can be used to organize facts prior to writing answers to essay test items. Help students select and use one of these graphic organizers to organize the facts they listed in 8-14.

### 8-16  Writing an Answer for an Essay Test Item

Have students read the guidelines for answering an essay test item. Be certain they use the graphic organizer from 8-15 to guide them as they write their answer to the essay item in 8-14.

### 8-17  Using QUOTE: Time

<u>T</u> reminds students to decide how much time they should devote to answering each item on an essay test while allowing time for review. Review the guidelines and have students answer the questions.

### 8-18  Using QUOTE: Evaluate

<u>E</u> reminds students to evaluate the content, organization, and mechanics of their answer in 8-16. Be certain students indicate how they can improve their answer for anything they answered NO.

### 8-19  Chapter Eight Mastery Assessment

Have students complete this assessment at any point you feel they have learned the study skills and strategies presented in this chapter. Review the results of the assessment with the students. Provide additional instruction as necessary.

# Getting Ready for a Test

Read the three statements to learn how to do well on your next test. The key ideas have been underlined in each statement. As you read a statement, think about how you would do what it suggests.

1. <u>Ask</u> your teacher <u>what will be on the test</u>. Ask what you need to study from your textbooks, handouts, and class notes. Also ask <u>what will not be on the test</u>. This way you know exactly what to study.

2. <u>Ask</u> your teacher what <u>type of items</u> will be on the test. Teachers often use more than one type of item on a test. Multiple-choice? True-false? Matching? Completion? Essay? Other?

3. <u>Begin studying</u> for your test <u>early</u>. Allow yourself at least five days to study. You will need at least this much time to review and master the information that will be on the test to do well on the test.

Use the underlined words to help you recall the important things you must do to do well on your next test. Write a summary paragraph that tells what you will do.

Once you know what to study for a test, begin following the five-day test preparation plan. If you follow this plan, each day you will find yourself more ready to take the test.

| | |
|---|---|
| Day Five | Review what you need to study from your textbooks, handouts, and class notes. Highlight or underline the important information. |
| Day Four | Rewrite the information you highlighted or underlined in the fewest words you can. Use these rewritten notes to review the information at least twice on this day. |
| Day Three | Use visualization, categorization, application, repetition, rhyme, acronyms, abbreviations, acronymic sentences, pegwords, and/or keywords to help you remember the information in your rewritten notes. |
| Day Two | Use your rewritten notes to make a list of questions you think will be on the test. Write answers for these questions. Review the questions and answers several times on this day. |
| Day One | This is the day you take the test. Review the questions and answers you developed. Do this once before you go to school, and try to do it another time just before you take the test. |

In your own words, describe what you should do on each day.

Day Five


Day Four


Day Three


Day Two


Day One

Here are five things you can do to improve your score on any test.

1. Read the test <u>directions</u> carefully. Ask for an explanation for anything you do not understand.
2. Examine the <u>entire</u> test to see how much there is to do. Do this immediately after you have read and made certain you understand the test directions.
3. Decide how much <u>time</u> you should spend answering each item on the test. Consider how many items are on the test and how many points each is worth. Spend the most time on the items that count for the most points.
4. Begin by answering the <u>easiest</u> items. Then answer as many of the remaining items as you can. If there is no penalty for answering incorrectly, try to answer all items.
5. <u>Review</u> your answers before handing in the test.

Use the acronym DETER to remember the five things you should do when taking a test. Next to each letter, write a statement explaining what that letter reminds you to do when taking a test.

D

E

T

E

R

There are two types of multiple-choice test items. Both have a stem and a number of answer choices. The first type has a stem with a part missing and is followed by possible answer choices. You are to identify the choice that correctly completes the stem. Here is an example:

stem       After World War II, _____ developed a plan to help rebuild Europe.

choices   a. Dwight D. Eisenhower
            b. Harry S. Truman
            c. George Patton
            d. George C. Marshall

The second type has a stem followed by answer choices. You are to identify the correct answer choice. Here is an example:

stem       After World War II, George C. Marshall

choices   a. directed the Berlin airlift.
            b. developed a plan to help rebuild Europe.
            c. commanded NATO forces on the European continent.
            d. ran for vice-president of the United States.

Using the following, write an example of each type of multiple-choice test item.

Coal, petroleum, and natural gas are fossil fuels. A fossil fuel is an energy source formed from the remains of living organisms. They take millions of years to form. Today, fossil fuels provide more than 80 percent of the world's energy needs.

**1.**

     a.

     b.

     c.

     d.

**2.**

     a.

     b.

     c.

     d.

# Guidelines for Taking Multiple-Choice Tests

Here are some guidelines to help you choose the correct answer for multiple-choice items. Read each guideline. Then answer the multiple-choice items that follow.

- Read the stem and underline words such as <u>not</u>, <u>except</u>, <u>incorrect</u>, and <u>false</u>. These words give you clues to the correct answer.
- Read the stem with each possible answer choice to decide which one to choose.
- When you decide an answer choice is not correct, draw a line through it.
- Do not change your answer unless you are certain you made the wrong choice. Your first answer is most often correct.

Circle the best answer choice for each item.

1. _____ an answer choice when you decide it is incorrect.

   a. Choose

   b. Reread

   c. Rewrite

   d. Cross out

2. Change an answer only when you are sure it is

   a. too long.

   b. too short.

   c. the wrong choice.

   d. correct.

3. You should _____ important words in a stem.

   a. underline

   b. ignore

   c. cross out

   d. look up

4. Read the _____ with each answer choice to decide which choice is correct.

   a. first word in the item

   b. last word in the item

   c. stem

   d. longest word

Read these additional guidelines for answering multiple-choice test items. Then answer the test items that follow.

- Answer all items unless there is a penalty for guessing.
- If two answer choices are opposites, one is likely to be correct.
- An answer choice is likely to be incorrect if it contains an absolute term such as <u>all</u>, <u>none</u>, <u>always</u>, or <u>never</u>.
- An answer choice is likely to be correct if it includes language used by your teacher or found in your text.

Circle the best answer.

1. An answer choice containing the word _____ is usually incorrect.

    a. sometimes

    b. usually

    c. always

    d. rarely

2. Do not answer items you are unsure about when

    a. you are running out of time.

    b. the item is difficult.

    c. the item is confusing.

    d. there is a penalty for wrong answers.

3. When two answer choices are _____, one of them is probably correct.

    a. parallel

    b. opposites

    c. complicated

    d. long

4. An answer choice is probably correct if it contains

    a. words found in popular magazines.

    b. language used by your teacher.

    c. information from a newspaper.

    d. words you do not understand.

Here are some guidelines for improving your score on a true/false test.

1. Choose FALSE if any part of a statement is FALSE.

   Abraham Lincoln was the first president of the United States.

   Why would this statement be FALSE?

2. Choose TRUE only if all parts of a statement are TRUE.

   Washington, Lincoln, Roosevelt and Kennedy were all Presidents of the United States.

   Why would this statement be TRUE?

3. Negative words such as *not* and *don't* can completely change the meaning of a statement.

   Washington, D.C., is the capital of the United States.
   Washington, D.C., is not the capital of the United States.

   The first is TRUE, and the second is FALSE. Why?

4. Items with two negatives are difficult to understand. To understand them you must cross out both negatives. Cross out the negatives in the following:

   You cannot get good grades if you do not study.

   Why was it easier to answer this item when the negatives were crossed out?

5. Absolute statements are usually FALSE. Qualified statements are usually TRUE.
   The sun is the energy source for all planets in the Milky Way.
   The sun is the energy source for some planets in the Milky Way.
   Why is the first FALSE and the second TRUE?

Use what you learned about answering true/false test items to take the following test.

**Test**

*Directions:* Circle TRUE or FALSE for each of the following.

TRUE   FALSE     1. A negative such as *not* can change the meaning of a statement.

TRUE   FALSE     2. Statements with a qualifier such as *some* are usually false.

TRUE   FALSE     3. If a statement has two negatives, you should cross out both before answering.

TRUE   FALSE     4. For a statement to be true, everything in the statement must be true.

TRUE   FALSE     5. If you cannot prove a statement false, consider it true.

TRUE   FALSE     6. Absolute statements are usually true.

Apply what you have learned as you answer the following:

TRUE   FALSE     7. All tropical countries are on the continent of South America.

Why did you choose your answer?




TRUE   FALSE     8. The principle of electricity is not important for understanding how a telephone works.

Why did you choose your answer?




TRUE   FALSE     9. Nylon, polyester, and wool are synthetic fibers.

Why did you choose your answer?

These guidelines explain how you can do well on a matching test.

- Read all the items in both columns before making any matches. One column may have more items than the other.
- Start by making the easiest matches.
- Cross out items in both columns after making a match.
- Make all correct matches before guessing at any matches.
- Make your best guess for any remaining matches.

**Science Vocabulary Test**

*Directions:* For each term, write the letter that shows its definition.

| Terms | Definitions |
|---|---|
| _____ 1. atom | A. breaking into parts |
| _____ 2. cell | B. organic compounds |
| _____ 3. matter | C. smallest part of an element |
| _____ 4. analysis | D. takes up space |
| _____ 5. photosynthesis | E. basic unit of all living things |
| _____ 6. hydrocarbons | F. how plants make food |
| | G. the study of living matter |

Did you read all the items in both columns before making matches?

Did you start by making the easiest matches?

Which were the easiest?

Did you cross out items in both columns after making a match?

Did you have to guess at any matches?

Which ones?

# Guidelines for Taking Completion Tests

Each item in a completion test consists of a statement with part of the statement missing. The missing part is shown by a blank line that can be anywhere in the statement. One or more words can be missing. You have to write the information that completes the item on the blank line.

Here are examples of completion items with the missing part in different places.

1. During the 1600s and 1700s, triangular trade routes linked colonial Americans with Europe, Africa, and the _____.

2. _____ were sent from Africa to the West Indies.

3. Fish, slaves, and _____ were sent to the Americas.

## Guidelines

Here is how to do well on a completion test.

- Read the statement and *think of what is missing.*
- Write an *answer* that *fits* the *meaning* of the statement.
- Be sure the answer *fits* the *statement grammatically.*
- If the length of the blank lines vary, *use the length as a clue* to the length of your answer.
- *Reread* the statement with your *answer* in it to make sure it makes sense.

Use the words in italics to write a summary that tells what you learned to do well on a completion test.

QUOTE is an acronym that will help you remember the five steps to follow to answer each item on an essay test. The five steps are:

Q = Question
U = Underline
O = Organize
T = Time
E = Evaluate

*Question* is the first step in the QUOTE strategy.

Q   Ask yourself the Question, "What <u>direction word(s)</u> in the test item tell me what I have to do to write my answer?"

As you read the essay item, identify and place in brackets direction word(s) such as [discuss], [describe], [explain]. For example:

Europe and Japan both flourished economically after World War II. Much of their economic growth was do to trade with other countries. [*Explain*] how economic growth in both Europe and Japan was affected by trade with America.

Here are three commonly used direction words:

**Discuss** means to examine different points of view.
**Describe** means to present a detailed picture of something.
**Explain** means to give the reasons for something.

Bracket [   ] the direction word(s) in each of the following essay items.

Acids, bases, and salts have unique characteristics. Yet they are related to each other in some important ways. Explain the relationship between acids, bases, and salts.
After examining a stereo system, describe what makes a stereo sound system different from a mono system.
Global warming is a controversial topic among scientists. Discuss the major points of view regarding this controversial topic.

Use *discuss, describe,* or *explain* to write an essay item on a topic of your choice. Bracket [ ] the direction word.

Here are more direction words you will find in essay test items. Sometimes you may see a different form of the word.

**List** means to present information in some order, such as 1, 2, 3, or A, B, C.
**Trace** means to state a series of things in some logical order, such as by dates or time.
**Relate** means to show how two or more things are connected.
**Diagram** or **illustrate** means to show examples of something.
**Compare** means to tell how two or more things are alike as well as different.
**Contrast** means to tell only how two or more things are different.
**Criticize** means to make both positive and negative comments about something.
**Evaluate** means to judge something using an established set of criteria.
**Summarize** means to state the major points about something.

Circle the direction word in each of the following.

1. What is the relationship between good study skills and good grades?

2. Use what was learned at the art museum to evaluate the painting on the wall in front of the classroom.

3. Make a diagram that shows what happens when cumulus clouds rise up a mountain.

4. Trace the important events leading up to the Persian Gulf War.

5. Contrast bacteria and viruses.

6. Develop a list of the ingredients you need to bake a cake.

7. Write a summary that contains the major events that led to the Persian Gulf War.

8. Write a critique of your favorite TV show.

9. Compare bacteria and viruses.

U  Underline is the second step in the QUOTE strategy. After you have [   ] the direction word, Underline the key words that help you obtain a clear understanding of the essay item.

Europe and Japan both flourished economically after World War II. Much of their economic growth was due to trade with other countries. [Explain] how economic growth in both Europe and Japan was affected by trade with America.

For each essay item: [   ] the direction word and Underline the key words.

The Declaration of Independence is a very important American document. Explain what the colonists were declaring in this declaration of their independence.

Every year people's lives are affected by weather disturbances. Describe the major types of weather disturbances.

The Lewis and Clark expedition set out from St. Louis, Missouri, in May 1804. Trace the route used by Lewis and Clark from St. Louis to the Pacific Ocean.

Make a diagram that shows how cells divide. Be certain that each cell has half the number of chromosomes present in the original cell.

Weather is a concern to all of us. Weather conditions vary with sun angle and the rotation of the earth. Compare weather conditions at the North Pole and the equator. Be certain that you write clearly and legibly.

<u>O</u>  <u>O</u>rganize is the third step in the QU<u>O</u>TE strategy. For this step do the following:

1. **List the facts you know.**
   On scrap paper list all the facts you know that are related to the key words you underlined in an essay test item.
2. **<u>O</u>rganize the facts.**
   Use a graphic organizer to organize the facts. You will be learning about graphic organizers in 8-15.
3. **Write the answer.**
   Use the graphic organizer to guide you as you write your answer.

Read the following essay test item.

> You can find a <u>weather map of the United States</u> in your daily newspaper. The map can be <u>used to predict the weather</u> that can be expected in different places. [Describe] the kinds of <u>information that are contained in a weather map</u>.

Find some resources that contain the facts you need to answer this question. List the important facts here.

Here are several graphic organizers. Examine each to learn how it can be used to organize facts. Select one and use it to organize your facts from 8-14.

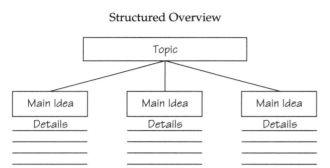

Structured Overview

The **structured overview** begins with the central topic. The central topic is followed by each of its main ideas. The supporting details are listed below each main idea.

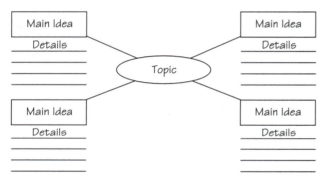

Schematic Map
Key Term and Four Categories

The **schematic map** begins with the central topic shown in the center of the map. The main ideas extend out from the central topic. The supporting details are attached to each of the main ideas.

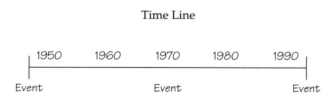

Time Line

The **time line** shows a continuum from one point in time to a later point in time. The intervals are expressed in time units. Important events are marked to show when they occurred.

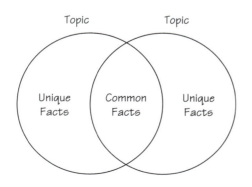

Venn Diagram

The **Venn diagram** consists of two overlapping circles. It shows what information is unique to each of two topics. The overlapping portion shows what information is common to both topics.

# Writing an Answer for an Essay Test Item

Here is what to do when writing a one paragraph answer to an essay test item.

Begin with a sentence that contains your main point.
Follow this with sentences that support your point.
End your answer with a sentence that states your conclusion.

Here is what to do when writing an answer of more than one paragraph.

Begin with an introductory paragraph that previews your answer.
Follow with additional paragraphs. Begin each with a sentence that contains your main point and follow with sentences that support your point.
End your answer with a paragraph that states your conclusion.

Using the guidelines you just learned and the **graphic organizer** you prepared in 8-15, write your answer to the essay test item in 8-14.

T   Time is the fourth step in the QU<u>O</u>TE strategy. For this step you must decide how much <u>T</u>ime you should spend answering each item. Here are some guidelines to follow:

- Know the total time you have to complete the essay test.
- Consider the point value of each item.
- Write in front of each item the amount of time you will spend answering it. Allow more time for items that count for the most points.
- Allow some time to review your answers.
- Make sure that the time you allow for answering and reviewing does not exceed the total time you have for the test.

Pretend you are going to take an essay test on which there are four items with a total point value of 100 points. The first item counts for 40 points and the others for 20 points each. You have one hour to take the test. Answer the following:

1. What is the total time for taking the test? _____

2. Which item counts for the most points? _____

3. How much time do you plan to use to answer each item?

     Item 1. _____

     Item 2. _____

     Item 3. _____

     Item 4. _____

4. How much time do you plan to use for review? _____

5. Does the total time you plan to use for writing and reviewing answers exceed one hour? If it does, what do you need to do?

E   Evaluate is the fifth step in the QUOTE strategy. For this step, you answer questions to Evaluate the content of what you wrote, its organization, and your writing mechanics.

Look at the answer you wrote in 8-16, and check YES or NO for each of the following.

                                                                                    *YES*    *NO*

Did I begin each paragraph with a sentence that states a main point?

Did I follow this with sentences to support the point?

Did I write a conclusion?

Did I answer all parts of the item?

Are all the facts I included relevant?

Are all my facts accurate?

Is my answer well organized?

Is my handwriting legible?

Did I spell words correctly?

Did I use correct punctuation?

Did I use correct grammar?

What could you have done to improve your answer?

See what you have learned about preparing for and taking tests.

1. What are three things you should do to get ready for a test?
2. What should you do on each day of the five-day test preparation plan?
3. What are five things you can do to improve your score on any test?
4. Place a check mark (✔) in front of each guideline to use when answering multiple-choice test items.
   If two answer choices are opposites, choose one as your answer.
   Select an answer choice that includes language used by your teacher.
   Select the first answer choice that looks correct.
   Cross out each answer choice you decide is not correct.
   Change your first answer only when certain it is not correct.
   Answer all items unless there is a penalty for guessing.
   Read the stem and underline *not, except, incorrect,* and so on.
   Select the third answer choice most often.
   Do not include an answer choice that has an absolute term such as *all*.
   Read the stem with each possible answer choice.
5. Place a check mark (✔) in front of each guideline to use when answering true/false test items.
   Choose TRUE only when all parts of a statement are true.
   Cross out negatives when there are two negatives in a statement.
   Choose TRUE unless you can prove a statement is false.
   Short statements are usually false.
   Remember that negative words change the meaning of a statement.
   Absolute statements are usually false.
6. Place a check mark (✔) in front of each guideline to use when answering Matching test items.
   Cross out items in both columns after making a match.
   Make the easiest matches first.
   Select items of the same length as matches.
   Read all items in both columns before making any matches.
   Make all correct matches before guessing at any matches.
   Make your best guess for any remaining matches.
7. Place a check mark (✔) in front of each guideline to use when answering Completion test items.
   Be certain your answer fits grammatically into a statement.
   Use the length of a blank line as a clue to the length of an answer.
   Read a statement and think of what is missing.
   Read a statement with your answer to make sure it make sense.
   Be certain your answer contains more than one word.
   Write an answer that fits the meaning of the statement.
8. Next to each letter of the QUOTE strategy, write what the letter stands for.
   Q
   U
   O
   T
   E

**8-1** Paragraph should include the following:
1. Ask my teacher what will and will not be on the test.
2. Ask my teacher what type of items will be on the test.
3. Begin studying for the test early.

**8-2** Day 5. Review and highlight important information.
Day 4. Rewrite highlighted information.
Day 3. Use remembering techniques.
Day 2. Create anticipated questions and their answers.
Day 1. Review questions and answers before the test.

**8-3** D = Read test *directions* carefully.
E = Read *entire* test to how much there is to do.
T = Decide how much *time* to spend on each item.
E = Answer the *easiest* items first.
R = *Review* answers.

**8-4** Students must write acceptable multiple-choice items for each of the two types.

**8-5** 1. d. 2. c. 3. a. 4. c.

**8-6** 1. c. 2. d. 3. b. 4. b.

**8-7** 1. Statement contains the absolute term *all.*
2. All were presidents of the United States.
3. Washington, D.C., is the capital.
4. Because the item is easier to understand.
5. The first item is false because it contains the absolute term *all.* The second item is true because it contains the qualified term *some.*

**8-8** 1. True. 2. False. 3. True. 4. True. 5. True. 6. False. 7. False. It contains the absolute term *all.* 8. False. The negative *not* changes the meaning. 9. False. Everything in the statement is not true.

**8-9** 1. c. 2. e. 3.d. 4. a. 5. f. 6. b. Remaining student responses will vary.

**8-10** Students do not have to answer the completion items. For your information, the answers are: (1) West Indies, (2) slaves, and (3) tobacco.
Summary should include the following points:
a. Read statement and think of what is missing.
b. Write answer which fits meaning of statement.
c. Be sure answer grammatically fits.
d. Use length of blank line as a clue to length of the answer.
e. Reread statement with answer.

**8-11** Essay questions students will write will vary. The direction word must be bracketed: [Explain] or [Describe] or [Discuss].

**8-12** 1. relate. 2. evaluate. 3. diagram. 4. trace. 5. contrast. 6. list. 7. summarize. 8. criticize. 9. compare.

**8-13** Students may underline more text than shown. Direction words should not vary.

The <u>Declaration of Independence</u> is a very important American document. [Explain] what the <u>colonists</u> were <u>declaring</u> in this declaration of their <u>independence</u>.

Every year peoples' lives are affected by weather disturbances. [Describe] the major <u>types</u> of <u>weather disturbances</u>.

The <u>Lewis and Clark</u> expedition set out from St. Louis, Missouri, in May 1804. [Trace] the <u>route</u> used by Lewis and Clark from <u>St. Louis</u> <u>to</u> the <u>Pacific</u> ocean.

Make a [diagram] that <u>shows how cells divide</u>. Be certain that each cell has half the number of chromosomes present in the original cell.

Weather is a concern to all of us. Weather conditions vary with sun angle and the rotation of the earth. [Compare] <u>weather</u> conditions at the <u>North Pole and equator</u>. Be certain that you write clearly and legibly.

**8-14** Student responses will vary.

**8-15** Student responses will vary.

**8-16** Student responses will vary.

**8-17** 1. 60 minutes or 1 hour.
2. Item 1.
3. Answers will vary according to how much time was allowed for review.
4. Answers will vary.
5. Answers will vary.

**8-18** Student responses will vary.

**8-19** 1. Ask my teacher what will be on the test.
Ask my teacher what type of items will be on the test.
Begin studying for the test early.
2. Day 5. Review.
Day 4. Rewrite.
Day 3. Use remembering techniques.
Day 2. Create questions and answers.
Day 1. Review again before the test.
3. D = Read test *directions* carefully.
E = Read *entire* test to how much there is to do.
T = Decide how much *time* to spend on each item.
E = Answer the *easiest* items first.
R = *Review* answers.
4. Place ✔ next to each guideline except:
Select the first answer choice that looks correct.
Select the third choice most often.
5. Place ✔ next to each guideline except:
Short statements are usually False.
6. Place ✔ next to each guideline except:
Select items of the same length as matches.
7. Place ✔ next to each guideline except:
Be certain your answer contains more than one word.

8. Q = Ask the question, "What is/are the direction word(s)?"

   U = Underline key words that help you understand the test item.

   O = Organize facts using a graphic organizer.

   T = Allow time for answering and reviewing.

   E = Evaluate answers for content, organization, and writing mechanics.

# Using Time and Space

## CHAPTER OBJECTIVES

1. Teach students a strategy for using time.
2. Teach students to evaluate and improve their study habits and study place.

## TITLES OF REPRODUCIBLE ACTIVITIES

**9-1** A Strategy for Using Time
**9-2** Semester Calendar
**9-3** To Do List
**9-4** Study Habits Checklist
**9-5** Improving Your Study Habits
**9-6** Study Place Checklist
**9-7** Improving Your Study Place
**9-8** Chapter Nine Mastery Assessment

## USING THE REPRODUCIBLE ACTIVITIES

After you have distributed a reproducible activity, here are suggestions for its use. Feel free to add further information, illustrations, or examples. Wherever possible, relate the activity to actual subject area assignments.

### 9-1 A Strategy for Using Time

Discuss the importance of organizing time and work space. Tell students they will learn how to prepare and maintain a Semester Calendar and to prepare and use daily To Do lists. Have students read the information and discuss the contents. Then have students answer the questions.

### 9-2 Semester Calendar

Make a copy of the Semester Calendar for each month in the semester. For each month write the month and year in the space provided at the top. Fill in the date for each day in the small boxes. Duplicate copies and provide each student with a set for the semester. Guide students as they record the due dates for assignments and projects and the dates of tests and quizzes. Periodically check to ensure that students' Semester Calendars are accurate and up to date.

### 9-3 To Do List

Make a copy of the To Do list for each week in the semester. For each week write the month/date in the small box. Duplicate copies and provide each student with a copy each week. During the first few weeks provide time for students to prepare To Do lists with your help. After this have students prepare To Do lists at home each night before a school day.

### 9-4 Study Habits Checklist

Introduce the checklist and discuss the items. Then have students complete the checklist.

### 9-5 Improving Your Study Habits

Have students list any habits for which they checked "No" on the Study Habits Checklist. For each habit listed, have them write a suggestion for improving it. Have the students share their suggestions with the class.

### 9-6 Study Place Checklist

Introduce the checklist and discuss the items. Then have students complete the checklist.

### 9-7 Improving Your Study Place

Have students list any feature for which they checked "No" on the Study Place Checklist. For each feature listed, have them write a suggestion for improving it. Have the students share their suggestions with the class.

### 9-8. Chapter Nine Mastery Assessment

Have students complete this assessment at any point you feel they have learned what they need to know about using time and space. Review the results of the assessment with the students. Provide additional instruction as necessary.

To get everything done you need to do, prepare a **Semester Calendar** and daily **To Do** lists. Here is what to do.

## Prepare a Semester Calendar

Use the Semester Calendar to record the dates on which assignments and projects are due. Also record the dates on which tests and quizzes will be given. The Semester Calendar is your long-term planner and should be prepared at the beginning of each semester. Revise the calendar as the semester goes on. Take it with you to school each day. Use the Semester Calendar shown on 9-2, or purchase one.

Each weekend, review your Semester Calendar to see the assignments and projects that will soon be due. This monitoring will help you budget your time so you complete assignments and projects on time. Monitoring also keeps you aware of test and quiz dates so you can plan your study time.

## Prepare a Daily To Do List

Each night before a school day, refer to your Semester Calendar to decide what you need to do for the next school day. Prepare a To Do list like that shown on 9-3. For example, on Sunday night you would refer to your Semester Calendar and write on the To Do list things to do Monday. On Monday, cross out things as you do them. Add others as necessary. Carry things not accomplished over to the To Do list you prepare on Monday night for Tuesday. Add new things that have to be done on Tuesday.

You could use a system to code the importance of each thing to do. For example, you might put 1 next to things you must do and 2 next to things you should do but that could be done another day

Answer the questions:

1. What should you do to get everything done you need to?


2. What should you record on the Semester Calendar?


3. What should you write on a To Do list?


4. Why is it important to schedule your time?


5. Why is it important to monitor your schedule?

Month _____  Year _____

| Sunday | Monday | Tuesday | Wednesday | Thursday | Friday | Saturday |
|--------|--------|---------|-----------|----------|--------|----------|
|  |  |  |  |  |  |  |
|  |  |  |  |  |  |  |
|  |  |  |  |  |  |  |
|  |  |  |  |  |  |  |
|  |  |  |  |  |  |  |

| | Monday | Tuesday | Wednesday | Thursday | Friday |
|---|---|---|---|---|---|
| | To Do | To Do | To Do | To Do | To Do |
| **AM** | | | | | |
| **PM** | | | | | |
| **Eve** | | | | | |

You need good study habits to get good grades. Good grades just don't happen—they come as a result of good study habits. Use the following checklist to see how good your study habits are. Read each statement describing a study habit and for each check (✔) "Yes" or "No."

| *Statement* | *Yes* | *No* |
|---|---|---|
| I have a planned study time. | | |
| I tell my friends not to call me during my study time. | | |
| I start working on time. | | |
| I review my notes before beginning an assignment. | | |
| I begin with the hardest assignment. | | |
| I finish one assignment before going on to another. | | |
| I take short breaks when I feel tired. | | |
| I avoid daydreaming. | | |
| I have a "study buddy" I can contact when I get stuck. | | |
| I write down questions I will need to ask my teacher. | | |
| I keep working on long-term assignments. | | |

List the study habits you need to improve in order to get better grades. Include any study habit for which you checked "No" when completing the Study Skills Checklist on 9-4. For each one listed, write something you can do to improve this study habit.

Study habit to be improved:

Suggestion for improving it:

Study habit to be improved:

Suggestion for improving it:

Study habit to be improved:

Suggestion for improving it:

Study habit to be improved:

Suggestion for improving it:

Study habit to be improved:

Suggestion for improving it:

Study habit to be improved:

Suggestion for improving it:

# Study Place Checklist

You need a good study place at home. How you arrange your study place has a lot to do with how well you will study and learn. If your study place is a noisy, busy place that is full of distractions, you will not learn much. If there is a telephone, radio, stereo, or television nearby, the temptation to use them may be too much. Thinking about people to call, songs to listen to, or programs to watch takes time away from studying. Time away from studying lowers your grades.

Evaluate your study place at home using the following checklist. Read each statement describing a feature of your study place and for each check (✔) "Yes" or "No."

| *Statement* | *Yes* | *No* |
|---|---|---|
| It is quiet. | | |
| There are no visual distractions. | | |
| There is good light. | | |
| The temperature is comfortable. | | |
| There is a comfortable chair. | | |
| It contains all necessary work materials. | | |
| It contains all necessary reference sources. | | |
| It contains a desk or table large enough to work at comfortably. | | |
| It contains adequate storage space. | | |
| I can use this study place whenever I need it. | | |

# Improving Your Study Place

List the features that need to be improved in your study place. Include any feature for which you checked "No" when completing the Study Place Checklist on 9-6. For each one listed, write something you can do to improve this feature of your study place.

Feature that needs to be improved:

Suggestion for improving it:

Feature that needs to be improved:

Suggestion for improving it:

Feature that needs to be improved:

Suggestion for improving it:

Feature that needs to be improved:

Suggestion for improving it:

Feature that needs to be improved:

Suggestion for improving it:

Feature that needs to be improved:

Suggestion for improving it:

Copyright © 1997 by Allyn and Bacon

**Directions.** Show what you have learned about using time and space by writing an answer for each of the following:

1. Why are the Semester Calendar and To Do lists effective tools for managing time?

2. How would you advise a fellow student to prepare and use a semester calendar?

3. Explain the procedures for recording and using information on a To Do list.

4. Write five good study habits you should have.

5. Write five features that should be true about your study place.

## ANSWERS FOR CHAPTER NINE REPRODUCIBLE ACTIVITIES

**9-1** 1. Prepare a Semester Calendar and To Do lists.
2. Assignments, projects, tests, quizzes.
3. Things to do the next day.
4. To know when things have to be accomplished.
5. To allow enough time to prepare for things that have to be accomplished.

**9-2** Students must complete and maintain a Semester Calendar.

**9-3** Students must complete and use To Do lists.

**9-4** Answers will vary.

**9-5** Answers will vary.

**9-6** Answers will vary.

**9-7** Answers will vary.

**9-8** 1. Student responses should include the following ideas: allows students to see semester goals, and make daily plans to accomplish what has to be done on a daily basis to achieve semester goals.
2. Student responses should include the following ideas: preparation at beginning of semester, recording due dates for assignments and projects, and dates of tests and quizzes.
3. Student responses should include the following ideas: refer to semester calendar each night before a school day, list things to be done the next day, add new things as the day goes on, cross out things as they are done, move things not done to the next To Do list.
4. Answers will vary but should include items from 9-5.
5. Answers will vary but should include items from 9-7.

# Bibliography

Anderson, O., & Kober, F. (1988). *Reading and study skills for the urban college student.* Dubuque, IA: Kendall/Hunt.

Apps, J. W. (1990). *Study skills for today's college student.* New York: McGraw-Hill.

Bleakley, A., & Carrigan, J. (1994). *Resource-based learning activities: Information literacy for high school students.* Chicago: American Library Association.

Bradley, A. (1983). *Taking note of college study skills.* Glenview, IL: Scott, Foresman.

Bragstad, B. J., & Stumpf, S. M. (1986). *Guidebook for teaching study skills and motivation.* Boston: Allyn and Bacon.

Chappie, E. *Smart studying four hundred.* (1992) Johnston, PA: Stoney Creek.

Chickering, A. W., & Schlossberg, N. K. (1995). *Getting the most out of college.* Boston: Allyn and Bacon.

College Board. (1991). *Student survival guide.* New York: College Board Publications.

Conan, M., & Heavers, K. (1994). *What you need to know about developing study skills, taking notes and tests, using dictionaries and libraries.* Lincolnwood, IL: National Textbook Company.

Crawford, J. W. (1981). *Steps to success: A study skills handbook.* Dubuque, IA: Kendall/Hunt.

Devine, T. G. (1981). *Teaching study skills.* Boston: Allyn and Bacon.

Devine, T. G., & Meagher, L. D. (1989). *Mastering study skills.* Englewood Cliffs, NJ: Prentice-Hall.

Ellis, D. (1994). *Becoming a master student,* 7th ed. Rapid City, SD: Houghton Mifflin.

Falkenberg, P. R. (1994). *Fifteen days to study power—The do-it-yourself study skills course for high school and college students,* 3rd ed. Winston-Salem, NC: Greencrest.

Ferrett, S. K., & Friedheim, J. (1995). *Connections study skills for college and career success.* Burr Ridge, IL: Irwin Mirror Press.

Forgan, H. W., & Mangrum, C. T. II. (1989). *Teaching content area reading skills,* 4th ed. Columbus, OH: Merrill.

Frank, S. (1996). *The everything study book.* Holbrook, MA: Adams Media Corporation.

Friday, R. A. (1988). *Create your college success.* Belmont, CA: Wadsworth.

Gardner, L. J., & Jeweler, A. J. (1995). *Your college experience,* 2nd ed. Belmont, CA: Wadsworth.

Greene, L. J., & Jones-Bamman, L. (1985). *Getting smarter.* Belmont, CA: Fearon Education.

Hamachek, A. L. (1995). *Coping with college.* Boston: Allyn and Bacon.

Hatch, C. C. (1996). *Student success strategies.* Fort Worth, TX: Harcourt, Brace.

Hoover, J. J. (1988). *Teaching handicapped children study skills,* 2nd ed. Lindale, TX: Hamilton Publications.

Hoover, J. J., & Patton, J. R. (1995). *Teaching students with learning problems to use study skills.* Austin, TX: Pro-Ed.

Kanar, C. C. (1991). *The confident student.* Boston: Houghton Mifflin.

Knight, T. O. (1993). *Study strategies for college.* Homewood, IL: Richard D. Irwin.

Kornhauser, A. W., & Enerson, D. M. (1993). *How to study for high-school and college students* (3rd ed.). Chicago: University of Chicago Press.

Landmark College. (1993). *Teaching a study skills system that works.* Putney, VT: Landmark College.

Leamnson, R. N. (1995). *Learning your way through college.* Belmont, CA: Wadsworth.

Longman, D. G., & Atkinson, R. H. (1995). *College learning and study skills.* St. Paul, MN: West.

Longman, D. G., & Atkinson, R. H. (1993). *Study methods and reading techniques.* St. Paul, MN: West.

Lovitt, T. C. (1991). *Preventing school dropouts.* Austin, TX: Pro-Ed.

Mastropieri, M. A., & Scruggs, T. E. (1991). *Teaching students ways to remember.* Cambridge, MA: Brookline Books.

McCarney, S. B., & Tucci, J. K. (1991). *Study skills for students in our schools.* Columbia, MO: Hawthorne Educational Services.

McWhorter, K. T. (1995). *Study and critical thinking skills in college* (2nd ed.). New York: HarperCollins.

Mensching, T. E. (1990). *Coping with information illiteracy: bibliographic instruction for the information age.* Ann Arbor, MI: Pierian Press.

Pauk, W. (1984). *How to study in college* (3rd ed.). Boston: Houghton Mifflin.

Rathus, S. A., & Fichner-Rathus, L. (1994). *Making the most out of college.* Englewood Cliffs, NJ: Prentice-Hall.

Rafoth, M. A., & DeFabo, L. (1990). *Study skills.* Washington, DC: National Education Association.

Robinson, F. P. (1970). *Effective study.* New York: Harper & Brothers.

Rubin, D. (1991). *Teaching reading and study skills in content areas.* Boston: Allyn and Bacon.

Scruggs, T. E., & Mastropieri, M. A. (1992). *Teaching test-taking skills.* Cambridge, MA: Brookline Books.

Sedita, J. (1989). *Landmark study skills guide.* Prides Crossing, MA: Landmark Foundation.

Semones, J. K. (1991). *Effective study skills: A step-by-step system for achieving student success.* Fort Worth, TX: Holt, Rinehart and Winston.

Singer, H., & Conlan, D. (1988). *Reading and learning from text.* Hillsdale, NJ: Erlbaum.

Sparks, L. R., & Sorrow, B. (1991). *Teachers and librarians working together to make students lifelong users.* Jefferson, NC: McFarland.

Starke, M. C. (1993). *Strategies for college success.* Englewood Cliffs, NJ: Prentice-Hall.

Strichart, S. S., & Mangrum, C. (1993). *Teaching study strategies to students with learning disabilities.* Boston: Allyn and Bacon.

Tonjes, M. J., & Zintz, M. V. (1981). *Teaching reading/thinking/study skills in content classrooms.* Dubuque, IA: William C. Brown.

Van Blerkom, D. L. (1994). *College study skills.* Belmont, CA: Wadsworth.

Walther, D. R. (1994). *Toolkit for college success.* Belmont, CA: Wadsworth.

Wolf, C. E. (1986). *Basic library skills* (2nd ed.). Jefferson, NC: McFarland.

Wood, N. (1995). *College reading and study skills.* Fort Worth, TX: Harcourt, Brace.

Yarington, D. J. (1977). *Surviving in college.* Indianapolis, IN: Bobbs-Merrill.